HELOISE has become a phenomenon
of the newspaper field. This fact is readily
attested to by the *Honolulu Advertiser,*
the paper that gave her a start. Its circu-
lation jumped from about 46,000 to
71,000 in less than three years after
Heloise began her famous column. Now
over 400 newspapers in the United States
and Canada carry her timely advice.
Heloise practices what she preaches, for
most of these hints come from her own
trial-and-error experiments; others have
been contributed by her growing host of
readers of her King Features Syndicated
column. Heloise and her husband, Lt. Col.
Marshall Cruse, with their two children,
now live near Washington, D.C.

A companion volume,
HELOISE'S
HOUSEKEEPING HINTS,
is now available in a *Pocket Book* edition.
Both were originally published by
Prentice-Hall and between them have sold
over 500,000 copies at $3.95 each.

Other books by Heloise

Heloise's Housekeeping Hints

Published by Pocket Books, Inc.

*Are there paperbound books you want
but cannot find at your retail stores?*

Heloise's
KITCHEN
HINTS

by
Heloise

ILLUSTRATED

A POCKET **CARDINAL**® EDITION published by
POCKET BOOKS, INC. • **NEW YORK**

HELOISE'S KITCHEN HINTS

Prentice-Hall edition published October, 1963
A Pocket Cardinal edition
1st printing .... July, 1965

This Pocket Cardinal® edition includes every word contained in the
original, higher-priced edition. It is printed from brand-new
plates made from completely reset, clear, easy-to-read type.
Pocket Cardinal editions are published by Pocket Books, Inc.,
and are printed and distributed in the U.S.A. by Affiliated Publishers,
a division of Pocket Books, Inc., 630 Fifth Avenue, New York, N.Y. 10020.
Trademarks registered in the United States and other countries.

L

Contents

DEAR FELLOW HOUSEWIVES   ix

1. STOP STOOPING!   1
2. TRICKS AND TREATS FOR THE TABLE   10
3. THE HOUSEWIFE'S HELPERS   40
4. FOWL PLAY AND FISH DAY   55
5. DO-IT-YOURSELF, KID!   65
6. MEALTIME MEMOS   71
7. BE A WASHDAY WINNER   93
8. BAKE-DAY BLISS   117
9. RISE AND SHINE!   141
10. HELOISE'S HANDY STAIN-REMOVER GUIDE   171

INDEX   175

Heloise's Kitchen Hints

Dear Fellow Housewives

This book was prepared with one thought in mind.

You!

Thinking of and doing for others should be foremost in our daily lives. In everything we do, whether it be making beds, doing dishes or cooking, we should do it with love.

The heart of a good household—the most sweetly rewarding part of woman's domain and family responsibility—is the kitchen.

If your kitchen isn't an enjoyable place for you, it should and can be! The secret is in learning to do things the easier ways. There is an easier way, a short cut, that can make most tasks more pleasant.

The best advice I can give is learn to "top clean." If something bothers you enough to make you nervous, then get up out of that chair and correct the fault—whether it's a drapery hanging crooked or the dishes stacked up! Don't let nerves get you *down*.

The pressure or thought of all of these hundreds of things we have to do each day is what causes "nerves." Nerves call for tranquilizers. Tranquilizers call for doctors! Save your money! Calm your nerves, and you can get things done an easier way.

You can save, too. Ignore what any neighbor may think of your cutting corners economically. She doesn't pay your bills or balance your budget!

You, the homemaker, are the backbone of the world. If it weren't for *you* there would be no home, family, or world fit to live in. *You* are a *homemaker:* chef (and many famous chefs couldn't please your family as well as you do!), nurse (ever kiss a child's skinned knee and he stopped crying?), court of appeals, peacemaker, home economist, purchasing agent, budget and record keeper, decorator, hostess.

How else would we have such wonderful experiences and outlets? The mistress of a home is lucky. Bless you!

You *can* laugh at your mistakes, *if* you learn through them! If no one made a mistake, how dreary this old world would be! Naturally, we all make mistakes. But these lead to improvements, and that's what brings about better and easier ways for which we are looking all the time.

Just because grandmother considered laundry a *duty* on Mondays, is no reason *you* should do your laundry on Monday, ironing on Tuesday, or baking on a set day. You are *not* grandmother. Do your chores the easiest and most convenient way for *you*.

If you do things when *you* are "in the mood," they are done better, quicker, and with far less tension and energy. If the notion strikes you at midnight to clean your kitchen, do your laundry or baking . . . then do it! You don't have to tell your neighbor about your idiosyncrasies. (However, this is a fact: she has her own! And probably more than you have!)

Remember: even though the grass looks greener on the other side, it, too, has weeds . . . when you look closer.

Don't try to keep up with any relatives, in-laws, the boss, or your neighbors. Just be *yourself* and do the best *you* can. And have yourself some relaxation and comforts! You deserve 'em.

Don't do without those simple, inexpensive items that will make homemaking and cooking easier. Spend a few dollars and buy yourself good knives and can openers; enough good pots and pans to cook a complete meal; and a few things which help so much to keep the kitchen a pleasant place to work in.

Get rid of the excess clutter in your kitchen. Not only does this give you more room in which to work but also makes for easier cleaning.

Family needs and schedules vary. Don't take all the suggestions in this book as gospel. Adapt them to your *own* needs.

Above all—stop working yourself to death!

I feel a closeness to all mothers and homemakers—to *you!*

I share that cup of tea or coffee with you every day. I only wish I were in your home, sitting at your table sharing it this day . . .

Love from the bottom of my heart.

Heloise

P.S. On second thought, let's have a second cup of coffee and have a real good chat about our problems—and our pleasures!

H.

1.

Stop Stooping!

▪▪

COLOR-KEY FOOD SHELVES

I have had so many requests on how to arrange kitchen shelves and in what order the canned goods go that I have tried my best to solve the problem.

I have kept a stockpile of canned goods all my life.

I have tried keeping them alphabetically . . .

I have labelled the edges of the shelves with "peas, beans, spaghetti, pineapple," etc. This is good and I have used this system many years, but it's time-consuming. For when you get ready to go to the store, it's hard to make a list of the things you need.

Then came the dawn . . . cook by color, so why not arrange shelves like that?

We know that when we have meat and potatoes we need something orange, green, or red. When we have spaghetti we need something green or yellow.

The main thing to keep in mind is that our cabinets *never* hold enough and no matter how many we have they never will. So I tried to find an easy and space-saving way for a housewife to find what she is looking for in a hurry besides a way to keep her cabinets neat.

Arrange all food shelves which hold your canned goods by *color!*

Place all of your "green things" on one shelf and mark the edge of the shelf "green" with a pencil, crayon, or felt marker. Anything green which comes in a can should be located on this shelf. Example: canned peas, green beans, asparagus and pickles. Yes, even pickles.

Here's why:

First, the average house has just so many shelves. Let's pretend you are making a sandwich. You need your pickles. Just why should you move catsup bottles, mayonnaise jars, relishes and bottles of steak sauce to find those pickles? No need to!

Just think: "I need pickles, they are green," so look at that "green shelf" and find your pickles in a hurry.

When you plan to go to the store and start making that grocery list, just look at your green shelf and see how many green things you need . . . and so on down the line.

Time is the greatest gift from God. What we save, we can utilize elsewhere. You need time to enjoy yourself. Think how many times a day you go to your cabinets to find something. If you could find it each time in one less second, and add those seconds up . . . see what you have saved.

Then spend that time enjoying being a housewife. That word is the sweetest in the world. Sit down and rest and think, "What a pleasure it is to have a few minutes 'stacked up' to do this one simple thing . . . Rest."

Here's the way I have arranged my own shelves:

Top Shelf: Canned meats and fish—these are for the days you don't have meat in the house and need a quick supper—dried beef, canned stews, tuna fish, canned lasagne, tamales, canned beef, canned sausage (that's a wonderful item) and anything which might be a meat substitute.

Second Shelf: Dried and boxed goods—biscuit mix, boxed custards, rice, etc. We don't use these daily so put them on the second shelf to save energy.

Third Shelf: This is the *green* shelf and the most often used. Put it where it is convenient and about eye- or waist-level. (Don't reach high for something that you use often when you can reach it at a more convenient level.) *Here* put your canned peas, pickles, green beans, asparagus, spinach, etc.

Fourth Shelf: This will be a *red* shelf. Put canned beets, tomatoes, tomato sauce, puree, paste, cranberries, pimientos, cherries, etc., here . . . about waist high. We use these things often.

Fifth Shelf: *orange*—Put canned yams, carrots, peaches, etc., here.

Sixth Shelf: *yellow*—Such as canned corn, pineapple, mayonnaise.

Seventh Shelf: *white*—Macaroni, apples, apple sauce, kraut, onions, pears, potatoes.

In another cabinet on one shelf (or a division of a shelf) put all your condiments . . . label it *condiments*. Here put your catsup, steak sauces, etc. (You can put your mustard and mayonnaise here, too, but being married to a MAN . . . he never can find them here, so I've found out. Better let him yell, "Where's the mustard?" and answer, "Look at the shelf marked yellow," and save your temper!

Label another shelf, or division of one, "spreads." This is for anything that goes on a piece of bread such as honey, jellies and jams, preserves, etc.

Then pick the most convenient shelf possible and put all your breakfast cereals here! Make it easy for the kids to reach!

Now . . . don't take me literally when I say "use a shelf" and think you have to use an entire shelf for this system. If you have only three shelves in your home for canned goods . . . divide those in halves or thirds . . . and do the best you can. The left half of a shelf can be for orange things and the right half for red, etc.

Then when you go to the store, it's no trouble to make a list or recall, "I am low on green things."

BE GOOD TO YOURSELF—REARRANGE!

Have you ever taken a look at the shelves under your kitchen cabinets, drainboards, and stove?

A mess, eh?

Well, let's take a few minutes and see what's wrong. I know you have been keeping house for years and it's hard to change, but after my 43rd birthday . . . I found the answer to those way-down-low shelves.

Rearrange 'em!

As we get older (and I wonder why I didn't discover this when I had those two young babies and my back was tired all the time), we see the energy we waste.

When we reach *up* for something it takes lots less energy than it does to reach *down!* Know that? It's true!

So why do we do it?

Habit! That's all.

Take everything out of all those bottom cabinets and put it on your kitchen floor.

Then stand back and look at all that stuff!

You will die laughing . . .

Here's a pan that you never use but just hate to part with because you have had it so long. Why keep it? It just clutters up your cabinet and makes it harder to find the things you do use.

You don't need 15 pans (and this is average!) anyway. You don't have 15 burners in your home to cook on! Ever stop to think of that?

Here's the secret:

If you are one who can't bear to throw things away . . . at least divide it! Put things you haven't used in a year in one pile and set this aside. (Later, put them in the attic or garage and if you don't use them in a year [chances are you never will] discard them.) Don't put these things back in your cabinet.

I like to line my shelves underneath the cabinets with foil. It reflects light. When you put a damp pan on foil and it makes a water spot it can be easily wiped up with a sponge. It's clean and sanitary.

Now take some antiseptic and make a solution with some water (read the directions on the bottle) and wash the inside of all your cabinets thoroughly. (It's supposed to be a fact that a roach or bug will not walk across this.)

If you do have roaches, now is the time to paint some bug juice on the cabinets. It's easy. They are empty and you can do it twice as fast. Besides, no use to do one cabinet at a time. When a roach finds one cabinet fumigated, it just runs across to the next one.

The shelves (especially if they are made of wood) should first be lined with wax paper. This keeps the foil or shelf paper from sticking to the paint. Then put your foil over this.

I always place two or three pieces of paper or foil one on top of the other when lining shelves. This way, when the top paper gets soiled, all I have to do is push the articles to one side, rolling up the soiled paper a little at a time, and replacing the articles onto the clean paper. Continue across the shelf, rolling back the paper a little at a time (and replacing the articles) until the entire soiled top paper has been removed.

By using this method, you will save yourself many hours next time you have to clean your shelves.

I also found, when lining shelves (especially those which contain canned goods and pots and pans), that if you will put a newspaper under the foil it will give a "cushion" effect and the foil lasts longer.

Those of you who can't afford foil can use newspaper.

Wallpaper is quite inexpensive, too. Especially if you buy "broken rolls" at your store. These are usually discontinued patterns put on sale.

Some women have written that they use bath mats, linoleum, oilcloth, or contact paper.

Now let's start to replace our pans.

First, use the "hidden" space in the back of the cabinets for those odd pans seldom used.

In front of those put all the other pans you use once a week or so.

Then pick up the ones you use most frequently. These will probably be a favorite skillet, a big saucepan, and two small ones.

Put one inside the other . . . and put these at the most convenient place in your cabinet. This will be at the front nearest the door of your stove.

It takes three, and never more than four, pans to cook a meal (remember, you don't have more than four burners and can't possibly use more), so keep this stack light.

Try to adapt yourself to new ideas. If we didn't we would still be boiling our clothes over a wood fire!

DON'T BE A COWARD—GET RID OF THAT CLUTTER!

Now, the stuff that we keep under our kitchen sink needs tending, too.

Get some newspapers. Put them on the floor and place everything in the bottom of your cabinet on these. The newspapers will prevent spots and rings on your linoleum and asphalt tile. Too . . . there is another reason . . . When you get through cleaning out, throwing away, etc., you will just roll up these newspapers and put the whole caboodle in your garbage and save more cleaning up.

Wash the cabinet with a disinfectant. Then paint on some bug juice. Let this dry thoroughly.

Don't replace anything yet. While you are waiting for the cabinet to dry, put some newspapers on your drainboard. Remove everything from that cabinet *over* your kitchen sink and lay it on these papers.

Wash, dry, and "bug-ize" that cabinet, too.

While this is drying, heat the coffee pot. Relax. Have lunch, walk out the front door and just look at the clouds. Anything . . . but take a few minutes off. While you are gazing, think: "Housework is so complicated. *Why?*"

Then ask yourself: "Have I got too much?" The answer will probably be "yes."

When you walk back into the kitchen, think again: "Now, Heloise says *never stoop when you don't have to*. Look at all this stuff that I have to put away. Why do I keep that bottle of bleach, the soap powders, the soap-filled pads, the ammonia, under the sink?" Your answer will be "because my mother did, grandmother did, and her mother did!"

"Why did they?"

Because they didn't have all the cabinets we do today. That's why!

All right, mama and grandma aren't keeping your

7

house. They aren't there to stoop for you. So why should you when you can avoid it?

Look at the pile of stuff sitting on your drainboard which came from your cupboard above your sink! What's there? Things you don't use three times a day!

What's on the floor? Things you use six times a day!

Put the bleach, furniture polish, soap pads, starch, ammonia, etc., things you use 20 times a day on the shelf above that sink. Saves you stooping and also has another reason . . .

Many of these items are poison. Did you know that?

You may not have a baby in your own home at present but your friends will come in with children and grandchildren. Babies love to open cabinets and drag out pans and bottles. Baby doesn't know if they are poison or not. All poisons should be kept high out of reach of small fry.

These small fry have taught me to save my energy, too! Bless 'em. Since I moved my every-day cleaning compounds above my sink I "ain't" had backaches!

What are you going to do with that "under-sink" cabinet?

Put the utensils you don't often use in it.

In most under-the-sink wooden cabinets and nearly all metal ones, I have never seen a shelf. If your husband won't build you one . . . build it yourself. I did!

You can get wooden boxes at your grocery store for free. (They usually are glad to have them hauled off!) If you are no good with a hammer and saw, just turn the box sideways, cover it with foil and you will have another good shelf and your cabinet will hold *twice* as much.

If you do know how to "knock-a-box-down" (that means take the nails out), use the wide boards for the shelf and stack some bricks under each end of the board. This way you can get the exact height you need and it can be removed when you move or decide to rearrange it.

But by all means don't have a cabinet wasted. Most of these are about two feet tall. Just who can stack pans or boxes of stuff two feet high? We need that extra shelf. Build yourself one. It's worth its weight in gold.

Ladies, this shelf under your cabinet should be lined with foil. It again reflects light! These cabinets are dark. I am well aware that you think foil is expensive. It is. But it needn't be wasted. It pays in the long run. It can be wiped with a sponge when it gets dirty and after using and reusing can be turned over next time you clean the cabinet.

Neither does foil absorb odors. The lightweight foil is good but the heavyweight is worth the difference you will pay, for it doesn't wrinkle as quickly as lightweight and won't have to be replaced as often.

I caution you . . . if you have wooden cabinets, put a piece of waxed paper down first to use as an underliner so that whatever you use as a liner won't stick.

Let's get our homes clean; get rid of all the clutter. We spend most of our waking hours in the kitchen. So keep it simple.

2.

Tricks and Treats for the Table

■■

WHEN YOU FEEL LIKE BEEFING

Want Tender Beef? Try Tea!

I have experimented for months with cheap cuts of beef and I feel that I have found an answer to a problem: how to use cheap cuts of beef and make them as tasty and tender as more expensive cuts.

Here's the answer . . . use tea!

Tea seems to tenderize cheap cuts of beef. After cooking chuck, boiling beef and brisket (I even mixed rib eye, which is ever so cheap, and it's great) I have decided that the tannic acid in the tea is what tenderizes beef!

Anyway, I take a big heavy dutch oven and pour some bacon grease in it.

Let this come to a heating point and put in your cheap cuts of beef. Let them brown until they are nearly burned. *This* is the secret of good gravy and taste! It also seals the juice in the meat chunks.

Cook any cut of beef you want, but I like to mix two or three kinds together to save time. Try brisket (which is practically all meat . . . not much fat . . . if you get the right cut) and rib eye, with boiling beef or chuck.

When all the meat is browned, pour two cups of strong tea over the beef (I use instant tea, no mess, no bother, and it's ready in a jiffy), put the lid on your pot and when the juice comes to a boiling point, *turn the fire down to simmer*. Do not salt at this point.

Let this cook slowly, nearly a simmer—for six hours. Sometimes it only takes four hours. Depends on how tender the cut of beef!

If the juices cook down add *no more* than *one* cup of water at a time. The addition of water will not change the taste of the beef.

At the end of the cooking period (I test this by sticking an ice pick in the beef . . . if it falls apart, it's done), sprinkle with salt and fresh pepper. Let cook another 20 minutes so the salt can flavor the gravy and penetrate the meat.

Now, as you add the salt and pepper, peel a few potatoes and carrots and throw them in on top of the beef roasts.

This will give you a complete meal. All you will need is a slice of tomato or a few leaves of lettuce to round it out!

And, ladies, do buy rib eye. It is wonderful *when cooked with other meats* and so tender. I do not suggest that you cook any of these meats without boiling beef or chuck with them. This is what I think gives the whole thing extra flavor.

If you have a small family, makes no difference. Buy one pound roasts (of different sorts) and mix 'em. Those who like lean beef can have it. Fat-eaters can eat the other cuts. But you and I both know that beef is better when cooked in a little fat!

By the way, these roasts can be seasoned with any condiment you might happen to favor, such as celery seed, Worcestershire sauce, catsup, chili sauce or even chili powder. I suggest that you leave these out the first time and taste the real flavor of the different meats themselves. You just might be amazed to learn what real meat tastes like! Many restaurateurs write to me, "Heloise, when I

see some people pouring catsup and sauces on my beautiful steaks . . . I die a slow death. These people don't know what the real flavor of a good steak is!"

USING YOUR NOODLES

Instead of serving potatoes with your pot roast, try adding more liquid than usual to the roast. When the roast is done, cook noodles in the juice. As the noodles cook, they will absorb all the meat stock and turn an appetizing brown color.

Of course, you will have to season the meat stock . . . the same as for gravy . . . before adding the noodles. Heap the noodles around the roast on a platter and dig in—delicious!

TRY CHUCK ROAST STEAK

From Connecticut: "I buy a chuck pot roast twice as big as I need for a meal. Then hubby cuts out the most tender portion from the center of the roast, and we broil this (after tenderizing it) for a delicious thick steak.

"I use the rest of the roast for a pot roast. We find that these steaks cut from the center of the pot roast, after being tenderized, are wonderfully flavored and as tender as the best steak we have ever bought."

From Oregon: "A beef roast (bone in or out) can be cut into steaks of desired thickness if of the proper cut. If boneless roast is too large around for one steak, I take my kitchen shears and cut the steak into two pieces, then I put wax paper between the steaks, wrap in foil and freeze for future use."

POTATO TOPPING FOR MEAT LOAF

From New York: "For a quick oven-prepared dinner, make your regular meat loaf and bake as usual. The last few minutes, pile mounds of fluffy whipped potatoes (I always add a teaspoon of lemon juice to give them tang) on top of the meat, turn down the oven and let the potatoes get a light brown. Sprinkle parmesan cheese on top. Really different and unusual."

From Kentucky: "I use a wire potato masher to decorate the top of my meat loaf and for fluting the edge of piecrust and cookies. Terrific!"

From Ohio: "I keep meat loaf from cracking while baking by dipping my hand in cold water and rubbing the top of the meat until it is smooth before putting it in the oven."

HAMBURGER HINTS

From Philadelphia: "When making hamburgers in my hamburger press, I keep the meat from sticking to the press by using paper cup cake cups. These are especially nice both for freezing and carrying hamburgers to the broiler. They are round and very inexpensive. (By the way, a hamburger press is a wonderful gadget to own.)"

Here's another good use for your ice-cream dipper: Use the dipper to make uniform meat balls or meat patties. If you like the deluxe-size burgers, use two dippers full of meat and pat them out separately. Then mash the edges of the two patties together.

For meat patties, use the closed end of a No. 2½ can to mash the patties flat and the open end to trim around the patties so they will be perfectly round. (Just as one uses a biscuit cutter.) Patties look better, cook better, and will have no frayed edges.

From Denver: "Want a good way to make lots of hamburgers for the crowd?

"Place the meat patties in a baking pan which has been lined with foil, place another piece of foil over them, put more patties in, place another piece of foil, add more patties and stack them up four deep with a sheet of foil separating each layer.

"The heat conducts so well that all of the patties will be cooked completely through in about 35 minutes in a 350° oven. Frankfurters may be done the same way, except that it takes only fifteen minutes."

From Washington: "Here is a neat trick for those who want a new taste in hamburger and meat loaf. For each two pounds of ground hamburger meat, add one can of tomato aspic! For the hamburgers, no egg is necessary.

"For the meat loaf, add your eggs and other condiments as usual. Use a little less liquid in the mixture as the aspic suffices for some of it."

If your family is not fond of vegetables, save any bits of leftover peas, carrots, etc., and mash them up fine when you mix your meat loaf, or fix hamburger patties, and add the vegetables to the hamburger mixture.

To make juicy hamburger and meat loaf . . . whip one egg white until it is stiff and add to each pound of ground beef. Fold this into the beef mixture and you will find the hamburgers will be light and juicy even when well done.

From Boston: "Many are the times I've found myself going to the refrigerator too near supper time to pull out a solid-frozen pound of ground chuck.

"Now, when I bring my ground chuck home from the market I freeze it differently. Instead of the square chunk, I flatten it between two sheets of waxed paper. Then freeze.

"When I want to use this ground meat for meals, it thaws much faster. Sometimes I pop it right into the broiler with a mixture of chopped onions, catsup, water, and a dash of Worcestershire sauce.

"This has become one of our favorite dishes. Flattening the meat before freezing sure beats chopping up frozen blocks."

WHEN YOU'RE IN A CHILI MOOD

From Colorado: "I make my own homemade chili by having the butcher grind my meat. Hamburger meat cooks into nothing and chili grind is much coarser. I use one tablespoon of chili powder and paprika with each pound of meat . . . and water to suit my taste.

"That is my basic recipe. Everyone has her own notion as to onions, garlic, tomatoes, etc. So use these to fit your own family's taste.

"I make 15 pounds at once. Why do it over and over? I put this in pint plastic containers (square to save space in the freezer). At the same time, I make an equal number of containers of cooked beans. Thaw when ready for use and cook separately and everyone can add the amount of cooked beans he desires to his own bowl of chili. Great for unexpected guests, by the way."

From Georgia: "Ever wonder what to do with a half-eaten meat loaf which is drying up in your refrigerator? I used it for my last batch of chili . . . which was wonderful. The meat loaf already has a flavor and after cooking it again, the taste is even better."

TENDER STEAK? BE A HAMMER-SNATCHER!

If you do not own one of those meat pounders (that's a gadget that looks like a sledge hammer and has a bunch of little squares on one end of it and is used for tenderizing meat) then try my method.

"Borrow" your husband's hammer! By golly there is no use in buying something and having an extra gadget in your drawer if you can get along without it. Especially when you don't use it too often. I don't see a bit of sense in cluttering up your drawer with a bunch of odd stuff when you can keep it clean and find your favorite paring knife.

Anyway, while I was preparing round steak the other night—I chicken-fried it—I could not find my "checkered sledge hammer" so I picked up my husband's new hammer. I used it to pound my round steak on my dough board. It not only served the purpose, but did a swell job. The *little* pieces of chicken-fried steaks all of a sudden expanded to a larger size. But . . . let me tell you what else I did to the round steak.

I used *unseasoned* tenderizer and let the meat stand for nearly four hours. (Gals, there are directions on the bottle which do not say to leave it four hours. This just happened to be convenient with me and made a perfect steak.)

I then put the pieces of steak in some flour and pounded again with my husband's hammer. This beat the flour into the meat itself. I put it in some bacon grease and browned it thoroughly on both sides. Put my seasonings in . . . covered it with the old lid, and after pouring a cup of water on it let it *simmer* for 30 minutes.

Ladies, please believe me, this is a grand way to tenderize your meat. Get out your husband's hammer. Wash it with hot water and a piece of steel wool and *pound* that meat. It's much better for tender eating!

From Vermont: "I save leftover pieces of steak, cut them into bite sized pieces and freeze them. I find that these are delicious when cooked with spaghetti sauce!"

From Idaho: "When broiling steak, I put one cup of water in the bottom of my broiler pan. This prevents grease burning on the pan and eliminates the smoke that usually occurs when broiling. This method also makes the pan very easy to wash. The drippings make delicious gravy."

From Texas: "When making roasts, instead of putting your slice of onion over it, take about a half of a medium onion and put it in your blender with about a cup of water. This will make a good onion juice that you can pour over the meat, and this makes wonderful gravy, also.

"I blend a couple of cloves of garlic the same way

for my pork roasts. This not only adds a good flavor all through the meat but it is wonderful when you have someone who objects to the onion or garlic. They never see it! You can add more water as you need it."

STOCK FREEZER WITH SANDWICHES

From a woman in Pennsylvania: "Our house is stocked with children of all ages—from 6 to 17. All are in school and take their lunches. By the time I feed nine children breakfast and each comes to the kitchen to make his own lunch, it is an eternal mess! I finally figured out the answer to this after all these years.

"After the family is off to school, I make up a big supply of sandwiches, put them in small plastic bags and store them in the deep freeze. I do this at my convenience.

"Now when it comes time for school, each child goes to the freezer, picks out his frozen sandwiches and plops them in his lunch bag. The sandwiches are frozen when the children leave the house, and by noon are completely thawed.

"This saves Mother a dirty kitchen every morning, plus all of the chaos.

"On weekends when I find specials at my grocery store on frying chickens, I buy ten chickens at a time. On the days when *I* am in the mood, I spend an entire afternoon frying all of these chickens.

"I put the pieces in little plastic bags, twist the ends secure with a rubber band, and put them in the deep freeze.

"One good thing about this . . . as each child tires of sandwiches for his lunch and prefers a piece of cold, fried chicken, he can see through this little individual plastic bag and know exactly which piece of chicken he is getting. It varies the lunch, makes it easier on Mother, and no more fights in my kitchen every morning!"

One woman wrote to me: "Sandwiches? After 40 years I should know! Leftover ham may be ground and mixed with jar mustard and a very little mayonnaise to make it moist enough to spread.

"Grated cheese mixed with mustard, mayonnaise, and tomato sauce is good.

"Cold meat loaf? Excellent!

"Try chopped hard boiled eggs mixed with mustard and mayonnaise.

"Use your own judgment on making up your mixture and add a little imagination . . . Try chow-chow, tomato catsup and so forth, mixed with enough mayonnaise to make it milder.

"Chicken, when ground, makes delicious chicken salad and it is always good."

From Texas: "I sometimes use a thin cheese spread on my bread instead of butter when making sandwiches. Try it. It's wonderful."

When making sandwiches for lunch boxes, wrap the lettuce and tomatoes in waxed paper, instead of putting them on the sandwich itself. At lunch time they can be unwrapped and tucked into a sandwich just before eating. Separate wrappings prevent the lettuce from becoming limp and the tomatoes from making the bread soggy.

Sandwiches made with mayonnaise do not keep well under freezing. Mustard or catsup can be used.

When making a batch of sandwiches for the lunch box, cut them in two before wrapping and mix two different kinds in one sandwich basket—for example, half a cheese sandwich and half a meat sandwich. The variety is enjoyed.

NO MORE SASSY SAUSAGES

Here's how to keep link sausages from spluttering and spattering over the stove when frying:

Cut the sausages apart and put them in a cooking pot big enough so that they can be covered with cold water. Place this over the burner on medium heat and just barely bring to a boil.

Take pot from the fire, place in the kitchen sink and run cold water over the sausages until they are completely cold. Then place in a colander and let drain until they are completely dry.

Put sausages in your refrigerator until ready for use. When ready to cook, place as many link sausages as you want to use in a *cold* frying pan. Turn on the heat and cook until they are brown on one side. Turn over on the other side and brown again. There will be no splatter or grease. When brown and hot clear through (avoid overcooking as this makes them tough) serve with a smile!

You can buy a few pounds of sausages at a time and prepare them this way. Then put as many links as you will need for one meal on a piece of foil, wrap tightly and put in your deep freeze. When you are ready to fry sausage for breakfast, you can take out one package at a time.

"JAR" YOUR GELATIN

I never make "every day" gelatin in a pan or bowl. I use a pint fruit jar! And here are the reasons:

I have two kids. They love gelatin so much, they can eat it by the bucketful.

I take a pint jar and put it in my kitchen sink and turn on the hot water faucet. I let the hot water run into the jar until it is very hot. I then dump out half of the water. Into this half-filled jar I pour my gelatin granules. I then take a tablespoon and stir it.

As soon as the granules are completely dissolved, I fill the jar up with ice cubes. When the ice melts, I stir again. I do all this in the sink. If the sink gets dirty or you splash some out of the jar while stirring, all you have to do is turn on that hot water faucet again, and you have no mess to clean up.

One more thing: if I plan to add fruit when the gelatin gets cool, I do not *quite* fill the pint jar up to the top with ice cubes. I leave about one inch or so of space. Remember, the fruit does take up space and you do not want to overflow the jar.

Place the gelatin in your refrigerator. If the fruit comes to the top of the jar, take the jar and shake it or turn it over. (But be sure that the lid is on tight!) The fruit will then distribute itself without any extra effort on your part.

If you do not have a lid for your jar, leave in the same spoon that you stirred the granules with. Place all of this in your refrigerator and as the gelatin begins to thicken, take your spoon and whirl it around to mix it up again.

Here's another idea that I hit upon recently because my two kids fought over who ate the most. Divide the gelatin into two small jars. This way each one can eat his own portion from his own jar. This has saved many arguments in this household!

Many of us make gelatin salads. About the cutest trick I have found, which can do for salads or desserts . . . is to use my muffin tin for a mold.

I happen to have a twelve-cup muffin tin. In *half* of the muffin tins, I grate carrots or cabbage, or both, and pour Jello in, making beautiful individual salads which may be topped with mayonnaise. The other half of the tins are plain gelatin desserts.

I just set the muffin tins on my refrigerator shelf for a few days.

So . . . one night I use the little molds for dessert topped with whipped cream. The following night I use those into which I have dropped the grated cabbage for a salad. Any type of fruits, vegetables, or pecans can be used for variation. Try sliced stuffed olives! Great.

This saves me the problem of what to have for a salad besides the old standby of lettuce and tomatoes. The gelatin salad is all ready, can be put in any plate immediately, and if some member of the family gets hungry in between times . . . there is always something to nibble on.

Grease the inside of the muffin tins with mayonnaise *before* putting gelatin in them and the molds come out easier!

Here is a timesaver when making gelatin desserts:

Dissolve the powder in hot water as usual, then add frozen fruit cocktail, broken in pieces with a fork.

While you are stirring, the fruit cocktail slowly melts and before you can say "boo" the gelatin is practically congealed!

START YOUR SOUP IN THE FREEZER

There is no reason to waste leftover food if you own a deep freeze.

Place a plastic container of about one-half gallon capacity in the freezer. When clearing the table after a meal, put all of the leftovers in the bowls into this container.

Include everything from creamed potatoes, gravy, vegetables of all types, rice, roast, steak, and broth from ham or chicken.

These leftovers may be added daily.

The food will quick-freeze in layers. After a few weeks of collection, depending on the size of the container, buy some nice soup bones.

Boil the soup meat with three or four medium onions until the meat is well done and falling from the bones. Then add three or four number 2 size cans of tomatoes and the leftovers. Let this boil for about an hour with salt and pepper to taste. This makes delicious home-made soup. After the soup cools, freeze the mixture in ice-cube trays.

When the mixture is thoroughly frozen, remove the cubes and place them in plastic bags. This enables you to take out just as many cubes as is needed for a cup or bowl of soup without thawing the entire supply.

When making my soup, I always add a dash of paprika (this makes it real red and rich looking) and lots of celery salt and fresh pepper. I have also found that if you do not like watery soup, some tomato paste can be added. It makes the soup thick and filling.

And don't forget . . . if you want the soup to go a long way and suffice for an entire meal, add some noodles, macaroni, rice, or diced potatoes.

FOR SUPER SOUP

From California: "I have found that an aluminum tea-ball caddy (the kind on a chain) can be filled with spices and immersed when cooking stews and soups, etc.

"After cooking, remove the caddy, and your food will

be free of cloves, garlic buds, bay leaves and all spices, but the flavors will remain."

From Tennessee: "Those last elusive droplets of fat can be removed from soup by dropping in a lettuce leaf and letting it remain until the grease is absorbed. Remove lettuce leaf before serving."

From Detroit: "Did you know that if you put ice cubes in a piece of terry cloth—such as a clean towel—and run it across the top of homemade soup . . . all the grease sticks to the towel and you don't have to wait for the soup to cool so the grease will come to the top?"

FOR A CHANGE—STUFFED PEPPERS

From Texas: "About the greatest thing I have learned over the years is to vary hamburger.

"Most people never think to make stuffed bell peppers. For those who do, I have a suggestion. Cut your peppers crosswise instead of lengthwise.

"This allows the pepper itself to be put in a muffin tin to be baked. Pile the meat loaf high. These little individual meat loaves are so pretty when (just a few minutes before serving) chili sauce is poured over them and allowed to drip down the sides.

"Another thing about piling the meat high is that those who do not particularly like the taste of peppers can have the delicious meat itself and leave the pepper.

"And, the best part of fixing meat in this manner is that the seeds from the peppers can be utilized. Put them in the meat mixture. Sure seasons the old hamburger!"

GOURMET OLIVES

Here's a real dilly for anyone who wants to serve extra-special olives. You can use ripe or green olives. First, open the container and pour off the juice. Put the olives in an old jar and add about one teaspoon of olive oil. If you like the taste of garlic, throw a little garlic salt in with the olive oil. If you don't like the taste or smell of lingering garlic, then use onion salt.

Shake the olives in this mixture of oil and garlic or onion salt. Let this stand at least 30 minutes before serving.

I also find that when you have a party that lasts two or three hours (and what guest ever stays only two hours like our invitation said?) this keeps the olives from shrinking and drying out.

ANYONE FOR CHOCOLATE TOAST?

For those who love cinnamon toast but eventually get tired of the same flavor, try mixing three heaping teaspoons of sugar with one-fourth teaspoon of cocoa and sprinkling it over buttered toast. Now what do you have? Chocolate toast!

Children absolutely adore this, especially when served with hot chocolate, which has been topped with marshmallow. They love to dunk the toast in the cocoa.

APPLE SAUCE FLUFF

Here is a simple dessert that is delicious and inexpensive:

Open a can of apple sauce and use your egg beater to beat it until it is fluffy. This may be seasoned with nutmeg or cinnamon. After it is fluffy and put in little dessert dishes it may be topped with whipped cream or a cherry.

I never waste cherry juice. I either put it in the whipped cream or mix the cherry juice with the apple sauce when beating it. This makes it pink and gives it an entirely different taste. What more can we have for so little?

TASTY TIPS

Did you know that you could add one sliced banana to the white of an egg and beat until entirely stiff and then add a little sugar and beat some more? The banana will dissolve entirely and this makes a wonderful substitute for whipped cream for those who are on a budget.

From New York: "When I ice a cake with powdered sugar icing, I always make a little extra icing. Especially the chocolate kind!

"After icing the cake, I put a little dry cereal in the pan with the extra icing and stir. Then I dip this out by the spoonful and lay each dab on a sheet of wax paper.

"Makes wonderful tid-bits! The kids just love them. There is no extra pan to clean as the pan is already in need of washing and these little drop crunchies suffice for the nights that I don't have dessert."

For those who buy syrup in cans, use an ice cream dipper with the thumb depresser on its side to fill small syrup pitchers. Dip, hold over pitcher and just "plop"! In goes all the syrup. Several plops and the pitcher is full. No mess, and it's grand in cool weather when the syrup is thick.

To get the last bit of shortening out of the can, fill it with boiling water, then let it cool. The shortening will rise to the top and harden for easy removal.

From Dallas: "When cooking or baking something that requires a number of ingredients, I line up the ingredients in a row on the cabinet, and remove the covers or open the container on each item.

"Each time I use an ingredient, I close the container or replace the cover. This way, I know I did not leave anything out . . . which often happened before."

If you keep a generous amount of ice cream in your freezer, from which you serve your family over a period of a week or longer, wrap the container completely in foil. This will prevent the ice cream from becoming icy and also protects its flavor. Rewrap the container tightly each time after it has been opened.

If you have trouble getting corn to pop . . . place the bag or can of popcorn in the deep freeze or freezing compartment of the refrigerator for at least 24 hours before using it. The corn will pop up large and tender.

CUT YOUR OWN CHOPS

From Ohio: "Instead of buying pork chops, I buy pork roast. It's less expensive, and of course I cut it myself to make my own chops.

"For Swiss steak I buy a chuck roast, cut it in half and prepare it for Swiss steak. It takes a little longer to cook but is less expensive."

From Maine: "Here is what I consider a different way to fix pork chops:

"Dip pork chops in cornmeal and then fry them until they are golden brown. Leave them in the skillet and bake them in the oven at 400° for about 45 minutes. They come out real tender and are not greasy at all."

From Ohio: "I save up about six or eight large empty sardine cans and use them as tins to bake individual crusts for meat pies. Children love their own initials on the crust! The tins may be used over and over again."

From Florida: "For those who want to know how to use leftover beef or lunch meat, put it through a food grinder. Then mix the ground meat with salad dressing, sweet relish or chopped pickles, minced onions, etc. Use this for sandwiches or . . . use ground beef mixed with cracker crumbs, butter, minced onion, and enough tomato sauce to make meatballs. These are delicious."

To correct lumpy gravy, just blend a little salt into the flour or cornstarch before adding water to the thickening.

From Montreal: "I have found that sometimes the gravy from my roast is not as brown as I would like it to be, so I add a teaspoon of instant coffee!

"This gives it color and flavor, too. I also put a teaspoon of coffee on top of my roast during the last hour of cooking."

KEEP A HAM HANDY

From New York: "My husband just loves to bring home guests for dinner and supper, and with a ten-minute notice!

"After years and years of being upset, I learned to always keep a canned ham in my icebox. I call this my insurance policy! Never is my icebox without a canned ham. Having a few cans of ready-cooked potatoes helps, too.

"Your ham can be served hot with baking-powder biscuits or sliced cold. I just wish I had thought of this ten years earlier."

When buying that center cut slice of ham—even on a once a month basis—buy it via a half ham and ask the butcher to cut off the first two slices!

It's much more economical than just purchasing center slices. And if you buy a whole ham, you can get *four* center slices! You can freeze either the center slices or the remaining two halves.

From Maine: "Here's the perfect answer to canned hams, guests, and parties!

"Buy that canned ham but let the grocer slice it on his electric slicer. Make some slices thin, some thick and leave a butt. Tie together with a string when you get home and cook as usual. When time comes to eat . . . place on platter and garnish, untie string and let those perfect slices fall into place like a pro.

"Why should we who have dull knives butcher a ham in hunks? And did you know that I have never seen a market yet that charged for this service?"

From Illinois: "I have learned that if you take a pie tin and line it with foil—crumpling the foil a little on the bottom—you can bake your breakfast sausage on it while your biscuits are cooking!

"The sausage will be moist, not hard and crisp, and it will have a wonderful flavor. We find it quite different than when frying it.

"The reason for crumpling the foil is so the grease can drip away from the sausage and stay in the fold of the crumpled foil. We find that frying sausage on a flat surface is what makes it greasy!"

From Louisiana: "For those who always have extra bacon grease and end up throwing it away, I have a hint.

"Wash any juice or beer can that has been opened with a beer-can opener. Pour leftover bacon grease in this can and you will have easy-to-pour grease when you need it for frying.

"The nice thing about these cans is the little rim around the top. It catches any slopping grease."

When a recipe calls for crumbled bacon, take a package of uncooked bacon and a pair of sharp kitchen shears and snip several times across the entire width of the layers.

You will wind up with a lot of "julienne" strips which will fry out into neat little "crumbles." These can be added to salads, scrambled eggs, sandwiches, etc.

From Rhode Island: "I prevent hot grease from popping out of my frying pan when I fry bacon by dipping the bacon strips in sweet milk and rolling in flour.

"It makes the bacon go further, it doesn't seem to shrink as much, and you also end up with nice brown grease for making gravy for those hot biscuits.

"It also makes the bacon taste much better."

When you buy cheese, cut it immediately into sections which will fit into a quart jar. Put the cover on tight and place in your refrigerator. It will keep for ages!

From Connecticut: "Before I grate cheese, I put a small amount of cooking oil on the grater with either a small pastry brush or a paper towel and rub a bit. When washing the grater . . . all cheese will immediately come off."

Cheese can be slivered easily for a tossed salad, welsh rarebit, etc., with a slit-blade potato peeler. For small amounts, this method is much faster and easier than grating.

From Chicago: "When I am making a baked macaroni and cheese casserole, I add one chicken bouillon cube and it changes the whole aspect!"

From West Virginia: "To keep macaroni from boiling over, I usually put a tablespoon or so of shortening in the water."

USE OVEN TO SIMMER SPAGHETTI SAUCE

From Pennsylvania: "Since making spaghetti sauce is an all-day job with me, I make enough for several meals and freeze it in proper quantities.

"Also, the biggest timesaver I have found is this: instead of simmering the sauce on top of the stove for the several hours that it usually requires, and the close watching and stirring to keep it from burning, just put it in the oven at a low temperature, about 250° (to keep it bubbling) for the same length of time. Hence there is no stirring, sticking, or burning."

From New York: "After spaghetti is cooked to the proper consistency, always blanch in cold water! This stops the cooking and keeps it from being soggy and sticky, and also washes the starch off the spaghetti itself.

"To reheat the spaghetti, just place some in a large tea strainer or colander and hold it under the hot water faucet for a few minutes (providing your hot water heater is at least 140°) or place back in boiling water until hot, then strain. Then tap the strainer on the edge of your drain to remove all excess water. The tapping will 'dry' the spaghetti so the sauce will stick and not become watery.

"Rice may be done the same way! Place in a big strainer after cooking . . . then tap the strainer on the side of the sink. Watch the excess water leave! This makes *dry* rice for your good gravy."

THE CARE AND FREEZING OF EGGS

So many of you have asked, "Can eggs be frozen?" This answer comes from a woman in Maryland.

Yes, eggs may be frozen, whole, or as yolks and whites separately when removed from their shells. Only the highest quality eggs should be used for freezing.

Top quality eggs, properly prepared, packed and freezer stored, hold their quality well for nine months to a year. For freezing use a rigid container such as heavily waxed cups, plastic or metal freezer boxes.

Containers should be small enough to hold just the

quantity of eggs to be used at one time or for one recipe. To allow for expansion of egg during freezing, leave ½- to ¾-inch headspace, depending upon the size of container. Whether to add sweetening or salt depends on how the egg is to be used, i.e., for cake or dessert, or for scrambled egg or main dish.

Whole Egg: Break into measuring cup. Add ½ tablespoon sugar or corn syrup per one cup eggs or ½ teaspoon salt. Stir with fork or beater enough to mix thoroughly but not enough to whip in air. Put through a food mill or medium-mesh strainer. Pour into container, seal, label, and freeze.

Egg Yolks: To each cup of yolks add 1 tablespoon sugar or syrup or ½ tablespoon salt and mix thoroughly. Strain, pour into container, seal and freeze.

Egg White: When separating whites and yolks, avoid getting even a droplet of yolk in the white. If a trace gets in, remove with tip of spoon. Otherwise whites will not whip well. Put whites through food mill or strainer. Pour in container, seal and freeze. No sugar or salt need be added to whites.

To Use Frozen Eggs: Thaw in container in refrigerator, use promptly. Once thawed, frozen eggs are highly perishable. Substitute for fresh eggs in recipes as follows: 2½ tablespoons whole egg for 1 egg; 1 tablespoon yolk for 1 egg yolk; 1½ tablespoons white for one egg white.

So gals, when eggs are on sale . . . buy 'em!
Watch for the ads in the paper and don't let this bargain pass you buy. Comes the time when eggs are about the price of gold nuggets . . . then enjoy 'em without choking!

Many people have written to me to say: never boil eggs (they should be slightly simmered) and never let them stand in the hot water after they have become hard boiled. This toughens the white part of the egg.

I believe this is true.

Here's why:

I took six eggs. Put three each in two different pans of cold water. I brought these to a boil and after the water came to a rolling boil I turned the fire down so that the eggs would just *simmer*.

After the eggs were finished cooking I took one pan, put it in the sink and turned the cold water faucet on, letting the water run over the eggs for about five minutes. (Eggs could be transferred to a pan of cold water and let stand.)

I peeled the three eggs from each pan. There is no doubt about it—the white part of the hard boiled eggs which were immediately put under *cold* water were absolutely tender. The eggs that had been rapidly boiled and left in the hot water had tough whites and were more difficult to peel.

I also found out that if the eggs were well-cracked and held under the cold water faucet and peeled while still slightly warm the shell removed beautifully without peeling part of the egg white off.

Another thing I found was that the shell nearly always stuck to a fresh egg, whereas with cold storage and older eggs this did not happen.

So, do a little experimenting yourself. Next time you boil two eggs, put one in each pot and test the two methods. See what luck you come out with.

When you plan to use egg whites for a special dish here is a suggestion to make use of the egg yolks:

Have a small pan of boiling water sitting on a hot

burner. The water must be at a rolling boil to keep the yolk from sticking. (The "simmer" rule doesn't apply here.) As you separate the eggs, drop the egg yolks into this boiling water, cover and boil until the yolks are at the hard boiled stage.

Dip the yolks from the water and let cool in a dish and store in your refrigerator. When it comes time to make sandwiches, mix mustard, salt and pepper and a dab of mayonnaise with the mashed egg yolks. This makes a he-man sandwich for a lunch box or a thinner spread for dainty lady fingers at tea.

From Virginia: "Let me tell you how I bake my eggs in muffin tins.

"I remove the crust from as many slices of bread as I plan to fix eggs. I then butter both sides of the bread and fit it into the tins. I break my eggs into these bread cups and salt lightly.

"Cover the muffin tin loosely with aluminum foil and bake. When done, your egg is already on toast!"

Break eggs one at a time into a cup instead of directly into a bowl. That way, if one is spoiled, you have not ruined them all. Or—separate them this way so that if one breaks, you don't have a yolk in with your whites.

When hard boiling eggs, put a drop of food coloring on each egg before adding the water to the pan. When cooked, they can be stored and the color will tell you which are the hard boiled eggs.

Or add the coloring to your water before boiling.

From Detroit: "My family used to complain that the whites of my poached and fried eggs were tough. A friend told me I would not have this trouble if I would remove the eggs from the refrigerator the night before using them so that they would be room temperature. I found this to be true!"

From Arizona: "I found the way to keep from washing that messy pan when making poached eggs!

"Take any coffee cup or small bowl, place a piece of foil in it and grease slightly (the foil will shape to the cup), drop egg in foil. When the water boils, pick up the foil and put foil, egg and all into the boiling water. No messy pan. Really, you do not have to use the cup at all, but can just shape the foil a bit so it will hold the egg."

From Arkansas: "Goody, goody! I found a new idea! When using hard boiled eggs to make egg salad sandwiches, or even when putting eggs in tuna fish salads and sandwiches, use your grater!

"It's fantastic the difference it makes. Saves time too. No big chunks of eggs to slide off that sandwich."

From Kansas: "When I fry eggs, I keep the grease from spattering all over my stove by sprinkling a little cornstarch in my pan. The cornstarch gives the eggs a wonderful taste and also the stove doesn't become a mess."

The best way to keep your cornstarch is in a big kitchen salt shaker.

From Maine: "My mother taught me a perfect way to fry eggs.

"I never could get a decent egg to the table, as it always seemed to crust on the bottom before the yolk was done. My husband prefers a firm yolk.

"Put just about one tablespoon of grease in a large size frying pan (use less in a smaller one) when the pan is medium hot. *Never* use a hot pan.

"Drop your egg in the pan, salt and pepper it, and then

add ⅛ cup of water and cover tightly. Cooking time varies with desired doneness of the egg.

"About four minutes will bring an egg with a firm center. Less, for softer centers. I do not believe any woman could have a failure using this method."

QUICKER BY THE DOZEN

From New York: "Heavens above! I have a family of nine and only this morning it dawned on me how to cook a dozen eggs quickly.

"Grease a pie tin (or two, if cooking a dozen eggs) and just break all the eggs into it and add a few spoons of water. Eggs will spread like cake icing. Put in your oven on the top shelf at about 350°.

"Just bake 'em! For those who like 'em soft, remove them early. The pan will keep them warm until the others are ready. If Pop likes his well done . . . let bake a bit more. Lots quicker than frying a dozen eggs and they are all hot at once, which lets Mother sit down to breakfast with her family. Use pancake turner to divide and remove eggs from pie tin.

"If anyone is lazy like me or has too many kids to get *everything* done, and *doesn't* want to wash the pan . . . line it with foil first. If *you* like steamed eggs, add more water and cover while baking. If hard, hard eggs are wanted, then break the yellow. Absolutely perfect."

EVER SEE A PURPLE EGG?

Why not try pickling beets? They are so easy. What's good about them is that they are cheap, quick, delicious, and can be used for many things—such as making purple eggs!

Buy a can of beets (I usually buy small, whole beets). I cut them crosswise in my egg slicer. They are then beautifully sliced, ready for pickling. Or you can put them right back in the slicer and cut them the other way to make long, narrow strips for garnishes on anything!

Now pour off one cup of the juice from a can of beets, put this in a saucepan and bring to a slow boil. Add one-half cup of sugar, one-half cup of vinegar, and just simmer until the sugar is dissolved. Pour the hot "syrup" over the sliced beets which have been put into a glass jar. (Five or six whole cloves are good when added to this, too.)

The best part of this recipe is that it takes no energy and anyone can afford it! The beets are grand whether served hot or cold.

If you have beets left over, place them in your refrigerator. Let stand for two days or more—the longer the better. When serving hamburgers or sandwiches next time, put cold pickled beets on the plate. And be sure to try these beets on top of plain lettuce when serving lettuce salad! They give that sweet and sour tang that will set off other food.

When all the beets are gone, save the juice: use it for hard boiled eggs! Drop the peeled egg in the pickled beet juice. The white part of the egg will get pickled and turn purple.

These purple pickled eggs are good when sliced in the egg slicer and placed on beautiful crisp lettuce, when you are desperate for a salad for your supper and are in a hurry.

Imagine . . . crisp cuts of head lettuce, a sliver of fresh tomato, a piece of celery, a few cold green asparagus spears (canned, of course), one or two stuffed olives, a few pickles on the side, all topped with your favorite dressing, and beautiful "sweet and sour" eggs. What a colorful salad!

Serve this with garlic bread or toasted crisp crackers. We go to restaurants and pay for beauty and something different. Why not make a salad like this yourself? You can!

3.

The Housewife's Helpers

∎∎

MAKE THE MOST OF YOUR ELECTRIC DISHWASHER

I have had so many requests and complaints on the subject of electric dishwashers that I would like to pass on these simple hints for those who have them.

There are many things that cause a film on glass: overloading or improper loading of your machine, infrequent washing, low water temperature, low water pressure, water condition such as hardness and iron content. Unapproved detergents and incorrect quantities of detergents can also be a cause.

The smallest amount of detergent should be used when cleaning glasses. Of course individual conditions should be taken into consideration when judging the amount.

If you have a portable dishwasher which attaches to your faucet—let the water run for a minute or until it is steaming hot before attaching the hose to your machine.

Some types of water will discolor aluminumware. Test whether you have a difficult water condition by washing a piece of aluminum to see if it becomes discolored.

Do not sprinkle your detergent directly on aluminum utensils or dishes. Put your detergent in your cup or sprinkle it on the bottom of the dishwasher before loading it with dishes.

Excessive water hardness may create a tendency toward film on glasses. Excessive total mineral content may cause water spotting.

Two things must be done to correct the filming and spotting on your dishes. Naturally, the film and spots must be removed first and then your improper operating conditions corrected.

To remove the film and spots . . . wash and rinse the dishes in your dishwasher with detergent in the usual manner, but do *not* dry.

Remove all silverware, cutlery, pots and pans, aluminumware and hand polish.

While the dishes and glasses are still wet, set ¾ cup of household bleach on the lower dish rack in a glass cup or bowl. Close door carefully to avoid upsetting strong bleach. Now, run the dishwasher through the cycle *without* any detergent . . . just the bleach . . . and do *not* dry.

Do *not* wash any silverware, cutlery, aluminum pots or pans in this bleaching step . . . *only* glassware and china.

After the bleach water has completely drained out *(without drying cycle)*, place a bowl containing two cups of vinegar on lower rack. Close the machine and let it run through the complete cycle again, and finish the rinsing and drying cycles in the normal manner. Do not allow the dishes to dry *between any* of these treatments.

I have experimented with these instructions and have had wonderful results. By using this procedure, you will not only get all the film off your glasses and dishes but the inside of your dishwasher will be cleaned at the same time.

One day I was at a friend's house while she was rinsing dishes before putting them into her electric dishwasher. She explained that she didn't have enough dishes in her washer to run it, so she always waited until it had a full day's supply of dishes.

This woman thought she was saving money by rinsing the dishes under the faucet. Think of the water she used!

I put my breakfast dishes in the washer . . . then turn on the rinse cycle only a few minutes so that this water can rinse them. Then I turn off my dishwasher.

I wait until the next meal and do the same thing. When the washer is full I run the washer through the entire cycle.

For those who have drying cycles on their dishwashers —there's no need to use the drying cycle if you want to save on electricity.

Let the dishes dry themselves by turning the dial to "off" after the dishes are washed and rinsed. Listen for the sound! Drying takes longer than the washing does. The dishes are already sterile and you aren't going to use them until the next meal anyway.

I never run a "half-full" dishwasher. I always fill it full: I use the extra space for seldom used glasses or china and silver. These can be washed, their shelf space cleaned and replaced in just ten extra minutes, rather than spending one dull day doing nothing else but washing and cleaning the china cabinet. Why wait until company comes?

From Connecticut: "I have found a few extra things that my dishwasher will do for me. Did you know that some light fixtures will fit into the dishwasher? This is a much better way to wash them than risking breaking them over the sink. Don't put plastic fixtures in if you have a drying cycle. Might melt.

"The most delightful use I have found is for washing my heat registers. My registers are the fairly small, removable floor types. They have cross bars that look like a checkerboard. These are real nuisances to wash in the sink . . . but there is nothing to the job in my dishwasher.

"I also put my drip pans from my stove in the washer every day or so."

SALT THOSE EXCESS SUDS

A woman wrote to me that when her dishwasher and washing machine were "overloaded" with detergents and the bubbles were coming out of every crack . . . she took a salt shaker and shook salt on top of the suds! She claimed that this immediately removed the excess bubbles.

I filled an ordinary kitchen sink with suds and hot water, using my hand to make all of the bubbles I could possibly get out of the detergent. Then I turned on the disposal. Naturally, all of the water drained down the disposal but . . . I was left with a sink completely full of suds.

I picked up a box of salt and gently sprinkled it over the top of the suds and immediately—if not sooner—all of the bubbles broke up.

I also tried this in my electric dishwasher. . This dishwasher is one place that is the biggest mess I know of when too much detergent is used or the wrong type of detergent is substituted, and it gets full of bubbles. (I had my dishwasher overflow with suds completely across my kitchen floor one day.) While the dishwasher had suds up to the top—and believe it, it's true—I sprinkled salt in it. The suds disintegrated.

Ladies, don't forget this hint. The day will come when

you will need it. Don't waste your time dipping suds from the dishwasher, removing the racks and all of the dishes. The next time it happens: remember that box of salt!

This also works in washing machines when overloaded with soap and detergent.

From Texas: "Recently, much to my dismay, I found I had used too much high-sudsing detergent in my top loading washing machine and suds were oozing out around the lid.

"Scooping the suds did no good as they just built up again when I started the machine. Recalling how bubble bath suds start breaking down as soon as one begins to soap down, I dropped a small piece of face soap into the lint filter tray of my washing machine and started my machine again . . . so the water going through the filter would wash over the soap.

"Immediately, those pesky suds began to subside and within a couple of minutes they were down to a safe level, whereupon I removed the soap and the suds stayed down for the rest of the washing cycle.

"I have also found that running cold water over a bar of soap will speed the breakdown of liquid detergent suds when doing hand washing. I discovered this when I accidentally knocked a bar of soap into the tub while trying to rinse out suds."

DON'T RUIN YOUR PLASTIC WARE

Please do not clean plastic cups and dishes with steel wool. This only ruins the finish.

The manufacturers of plastic dishes say that even scouring powders and bleaches will ruin them. Once the finish has been removed there is nothing you can do. They suggest using only baking soda or a special product made for this purpose.

To use baking soda, dip a damp cloth into regular soda and polish as if cleaning silver.

YOU MAY NOT NEED A REPAIRMAN

Have you ever looked at your garbage disposal unit under your sink? If you will look under the sink you will see a white gadget and it ordinarily has instructions printed on it.

The directions will say, "If your disposal quits working (and these will not be the exact words), wait for five minutes, then push the red button on the bottom of the disposal unit!"

Punch the button a few seconds, turn on your water, turn on the disposal electrical switch, and see if it works before calling the repairman.

Now, if your model is not this type and you do have to call him, stay in the kitchen and watch exactly what he does. Not only will you save a few dollars next time, but you won't have to wait until he can make your service call.

If you have a garbage disposal, some day take a flashlight, pull the rubber flaps back and look down into the disposal and see how close the grinding gadget is! Some grinders are closer to the sink than others. Don't take a chance on grinding your fingers away. Take your flashlight, and a few minutes of your time, and it might save you not only a finger but a knuckle, too!

NEW WAY TO CLEAN OVENS

Here is the latest on cleaning your oven with ammonia:
Heat your oven! Turn on the heat until it reaches 200°. Turn it off.

Let it cool until it is warm enough so that you can touch it with your hands and not get burned! There must be a reason for this but all I can figure out is that heat (when the porcelain inside is warm) produces faster and better cleaning by far.

Now get a bath towel (I use an old one but it makes no difference) and wet it with warm water. Wring it out well. (Don't ask me what this does, but I cleaned five ovens and found it works far better than a dry towel. I think it prevents the ammonia from soaking into the towel so quickly.)

Lay the damp towel on the bottom wire rack in your oven. Wet as many wash rags as you will need to plug up all vent holes in your oven. Dampness in the rags keeps the fumes in the oven and helps keep them out of the kitchen. But be sure to open the kitchen windows for *your* ventilation.

Now . . . pour ammonia over this wet towel in your oven. I used anywhere from one to two cups. The amount depends on how dirty the oven is, or how deep the carbon (the black and brown stuff on your oven walls and racks) appears.

Close the oven door and forget it for a few hours. Because the oven is still warm, I found that the vapors from the ammonia worked faster! If you smell ammonia fumes getting strong . . . perhaps you missed an oven vent somewhere! (I did on one oven. It had three vents.)

Soon all odors will leave. When odor evaporates, then start operation number two! But . . . let me tell you the easiest way I have found.

Before you do anything . . . remove that towel and one oven rack. Put the rack in your kitchen sink and lay the towel on top of it. Turn your water faucet over the towel until the water soaks it well. Then slightly wring the towel out. Wash as usual. It will be as clean as a whistle.

Now, get out some steel wool. I found it better not to use a soap-filled pad. A plain steel wool pad was better. I rinsed the soap out of the soap-filled pads under hot water to remove most of the soap.

If you have any great build-up of carbon on the rack, take the pad and gently rub. It comes off like magic! Repeat the process for all the racks.

And ladies, the glass door on my oven came clean as a whistle! No effort at all. I just used a sponge dipped in a little water to which some vinegar had been added. Complete magic! Then I cleaned the inside of the oven with this same vinegar water. Sure pretty.

For those who have very heavily coated racks (carbon again) I did find a better way to clean them. Fill up your wash tub or bath tub sometime when it's not in use if you don't have a sink big enough to cover your racks completely with *very* hot water.

Add about a cup or so of detergent. Plunge the racks *under* the water and leave overnight. In the morning you will find the "goop" has worked itself off! Most of it is floating on top of the water. The rest can be wiped off with a vegetable brush. Terrific.

Get up out of that chair! Clean that oven today. Oh, it will be beautiful, and remember to keep it clean next time! Use foil when you bake things.

From Montreal: "I just struck upon an idea of how to get rid of the peculiar smell resulting from some of these fabulous new oven cleaners.

"I peeled an orange and laid some of the peelings on the oven racks and turned the oven up to 350°. Before

47

long the whole house was filled with the delicious woody smell of the orange peel! I can remember my mother throwing orange peel on the top of her wood stove. Try some orange peelings in your fireplace the next time you build a fire."

From Florida: "I clean the glass door of my oven by dipping a washcloth in baking soda. I use this as one would ordinarily use a scouring powder. Wet the cloth and wring it out thoroughly, then dip in the soda. Scrub in rotary motion over the carbon spots. Works like a magic wand."

IF YOU HATE TO DEFROST SO OFTEN . . .

I have a regular refrigerator without automatic defrost. I do not like to defrost! Who does?

I tried to figure just why so much frost builds up on and around the box where I keep the ice trays. I started research. Frost occurs when warm air comes in contact with the freezing unit.

I have experimented with nine different refrigerators. All non-automatics have a space around that little door which flips open before you can remove an ice tray!

I decided to try to eliminate what frost I could . . . so at least if I had to go another week without defrosting, the door would close! The ice builds up so fast that sometimes the hinge just won't close!

Here's what I did:

I took a cardboard tube—the kind that comes inside foil and waxed paper—and cut it to fit between the wall of the refrigerator and the freezing unit.

This roll of cardboard should stand "upright" and should be just about an inch *behind* the clasp on that freezing unit door. Not too far . . . you only want to block the hot air and keep it from hitting that freezing unit. It will look as if you were putting a book on a book shelf and cramming it between two other books.

Here's what it does:

I have tested and found that when I open the door the suction draws the hot air in more on that side where the refrigerator handle is. This is the reason that the ice builds up on that side first!

By blocking the air with this roll of cardboard . . . it keeps the ice from building up! Result? Don't have to defrost as often!

Ladies, I have tried sponges . . . they just don't work. They freeze. They have no air hole (like the cardboard insertion) and the air won't circulate. Also . . . if you go an extra long time before defrosting and the ice builds up, the cardboard can be easily removed.

A word of safety on defrosting refrigerators and deep freezers:

You may not know it but this can be a dangerous job. *Always* pull the plug out from the wall socket before you ever start to defrost. It just might save your life. At the very least, it eliminates the possibility of any shock.

When defrosting a refrigerator, put several thicknesses of newspapers on the top shelf under the freezing unit.

By doing this, the ice and water which spill over will be absorbed by the paper and kept off the rest of the contents in the refrigerator. Makes the clean-up job much quicker and less work.

From Louisiana: "Opening and closing a refrigerator not only allows it to lose its coldness but Mother has to defrost it more often.

"My kids will open that refrigerator and just stand there for minutes looking to see if they want something. Most times all they need is a drink of water.

"I solved the problem and cut the time down to a few seconds by buying different colored plastic glasses and marking them (and it is most important to mark the individual glasses with names) with a felt marker. I use the first names and abbreviate them so that the child can recognize his glass instantly.

"Now, when a child opens the refrigerator door he immediately grabs the glass which has his name (if they're different colors he can spot it more quickly . . . thus saving more time).

"When my kids need juices I surprise them by filling each glass with some. And sometimes I fool them again by filling it full of milk to which has been added some chocolate! This way they get their milk.

"Last year I used soda-pop bottles. I found this even more satisfactory than the glasses because the little ones sometimes spill a glass of something. Somehow they can just hold a pop bottle easier than a glass."

THOSE STICKING ICE CUBE TRAYS

What causes ice in ice cube trays to stick?

Some of you fill your ice trays with hot water and place them in your freezer chest to defrost more quickly. Do not do this.

As far as I know, most refrigerator companies "coat" these trays. When you put boiling hot water in them it melts and removes this coating. Nothing should be placed in these trays except cool water. Also, they should never be put in dishwashers with extremely hot water or soaps. This removes the coating and causes sticking.

The only remedy I have found is: Use some sort of spray coating (such as is used for spraying fry pans and casserole dishes to prevent sticking). Dry the tray thoroughly and then coat it with one of these sprays.

I am well aware that these sprays are not sold for this purpose, nor do their directions mention using them for this, but outside of buying new trays, that's the best answer I have found.

If you will use the waxed paper which comes in a roll . . . and put a piece of it under your ice trays after defrosting . . . you will not have any trouble removing them from the freezer. Your ice trays will not stick to the bottom.

Have you ever been in a hurry to replace an ice tray back in the refrigerator—especially the type with the plastic inserts—and find that the ice tray divider is in backwards? What I am talking about is the kind which is more slanted on one end than on the other. Why they don't make both ends alike I'll never know!

Well . . . I've found the answer, gals. Just take a dab of fingernail polish and put a dot on one end of the plastic insert and put another dot on the matching end of the tray. This way, whether you are in a hurry or not, all you have to do is just see that the two red dots are on one end.

STOCK THE LEFTOVERS

If your refrigerator is short of space for those small and numerous leftovers, then do this: Place one layer of leftovers in the bottom of a container, cover with a small piece of foil and repeat the procedure until all of your leftovers are "stacked" in one container!

This way if you have three dabs of something, you do not have three bowls in the refrigerator. When ready to remove, just lift out the correct piece of foil.

A sheet of aluminum foil on a portion of the shelf of the refrigerator where you store your milk cartons saves much work later. So often one carton will leak. It is easier to clean the foil or change it than to clean the shelves of the refrigerator itself.

This foil also prevents the wax on the cartons from getting on the shelves.

FOIL KEEPS ICE FROM STICKING

From Pennsylvania: "I line all my freezer shelves with heavy duty foil. I find that this will cling to all of the sides and the top. Now, when I clean out the freezer, I just remove the foil and wipe it out!"

For months I have had my deep freeze shelves lined with heavy duty foil, testing this.

When the ice built up and it was defrosting time, I just disconnected the freezer and when the ice started to melt, it just slipped off in big chunks and slabs. It did not stick to the wire grates as it did previously.

After trying this, I found out there is a freezer liner on the market which is extremely heavy foil and was made for this very thing. Special tape comes with this to use when applying the foil to the walls and the top of the freezer. It is great and may be used over and over again.

REMOVE ODORS

When food has spoiled in a refrigerator, place a pan of uncompressed charcoal in the freezing unit and in the main body of the refrigerator.

Place fresh charcoal in each day and put the other out to dry in the sun to be used the following day. The charcoal will absorb the odors and gradually the odors will disappear.

This also works in deep freezers.

GADGET TRICKS

From Ohio: "I wonder if everyone who owns a blender really uses it as an aid. I use mine for loads of chopping chores, especially for onions and green peppers.

"I put a small amount in at a time and buzz a little, remove that, and buzz more, until I have the required amount for a recipe. This also applies to bread crumbs, soft or hard.

"The best thing I have yet found is using my blender for cabbage slaw. I always broke fingernails on my grater. Now I put medium-size pieces of cabbage in the blender —then fill it with water—buzz a little, drain water off, and repeat the process until I have enough slaw.

"This is one way to have the perfect slaw in just a few minutes, but it must be drained thoroughly before adding the dressing."

From Florida: "I clean the bottom of my electric skillet each time I use it. This way the grease does not have an opportunity to burn every time I cook something.

"I use a soap-filled pad and a little cleanser. For those women who have a 'build-up' on their skillets, they might try removing the legs of the pan and the job is done quicker and easier.

"This 'build-up' goes on one layer at a time. It must be taken off the same way. Clean it each day and prevent 'build-up.' "

From Georgia: "I use a plastic shower cap as a cover for my waffle iron. It fits perfectly, and looks lovely."

From Maryland: "I clean my waffle iron by making a paste of soda and water. I scrub the iron with this, using a toothbrush. Wipe the grill clean with a damp rag, then brush the iron with salad oil. Heat. Bake a waffle and throw the first one away.

"Your iron is now ready to use. It has been tempered again. Do not grease the iron again until it needs cleaning."

From Vermont: "When using my food grinder, I put a piece of sandpaper—rough side toward the food grinder—on the table and the grinder will not slip. Before removing the grinder, I run a piece of bread through it and it is much easier to wash."

4.

Fowl Play and Fish Day

■■■

TALKING TURKEY

After cooking turkey many ways and using many recipes I am going to tell you what I thought was "the perfect turkey." Not only was it less trouble but also it was the most beautiful. I steamed it as it baked by pouring a cup of water in the body cavity. This keeps the meat juicy.

If you like white meat, a minimum weight for the turkey should be about 20 pounds. If you can possibly afford it, buy a broad-breasted turkey. The better quality is worth the difference in price. Also, a turkey around 20 pounds is a better buy—you are buying more meat in proportion to the bone structure. In "broad-breasted turkeys" (the label will tell you if they are) you have more white meat. Leftovers may be frozen for later use.

Another thing that might interest you is . . . don't salt your turkey before cooking it. This will shock most of you who are in the habit of rubbing it with salt inside or out, but, believe me, it is better if you don't.

A 20-pound frozen turkey takes at least three days to thaw properly in the refrigerator. One may be left overnight on the drainboard if necessary, but too-fast thawing causes it to lose its good juices and makes the meat tough.

Remove pin feathers on thawed turkey with tweezers. Remove giblets. Carefully wash turkey inside and out with cold water. Fold skin of neck under the back and fasten with toothpicks if you haven't any metal skewers. Tie the ends of the legs with a string and knot it. Fold tail up into the cavity and fasten. Fold wings under the back with tips touching.

Remove broiler rack from bottom of oven and cover it with heavy quilted foil. Use three *long strips* in center of rack and place turkey in the middle of this. Pour one cup of water into the cavity of the bird. This will provide the steam as the bird roasts.

Take a brown paper grocery sack and tear a round piece big enough to cover the top of the bird. Rub the sack with lots of yellow shortening (this makes the bird golden brown) or another unsalted fat of your choice. Place greased side of sack "down" on breast of bird and wrap the whole turkey with the six ends of the strips of foil, making sure they overlap one another.

Place in 300° oven for at least five hours for a 20-pound bird. Reduce cooking time for smaller birds.

At the end of the cooking time open the foil, remove the brown paper bag, and let the steam and the heat escape. Move the tip of the leg with your fingers. If it moves easily, it's about ready to eat. But not quite. Dip a paper napkin or towel into the drippings in the bottom of the pan and carefully wipe the turkey with it until all the bird is oiled. For a dry, extra brown turkey, roast uncovered about 15 minutes more.

Sprinkle the entire bird lightly with paprika until it turns a golden color. Place turkey on a platter when slightly cool (it cuts better) and garnish with lots of parsley.

Make corn bread dressing with part of the turkey drippings and cook separately on cookie sheet. Use part of the drippings for giblet gravy made with the giblets which you have boiled separately.

Serve with creamy mashed potatoes, green frozen peas, celery hearts, cranberry sauce, and hot biscuits.

Naturally all this is served to hungry people who have smelled the aroma for hours and are starving! All that is left for you to do is sit back and watch it disappear. Then wash the dishes.

NEW TWIST FOR AN OLD FAVORITE

I'd like to pass along a recipe for Old Fashioned Turkey Dressing cooked by a new method—on a cookie sheet! I have used it for years and I have never found any better.

It's not really as complicated as it looks. And I found a shorter method for one of the ingredients than grandmother used. I bake canned biscuits! Can't tell the difference. I still make my southern corn bread but you can use any package mix. Cook both biscuits and corn bread at once and toast that loaf of white bread while the oven is on. These can all be made a day ahead of time or weeks ahead and frozen.

The recipe:

1 can biscuits
1 package yellow corn bread
1 large loaf of bread, toasted
2 eggs (uncooked)
1½ cups chopped onions
2 cups chopped celery

1 cup chopped celery tops
1 tablespoon sage
1 tablespoon poultry seasonings
2 cups water
1 cup turkey drippings
salt and pepper to taste

Break all breads into small pieces and put into a big pot. Set aside.

Put all the remaining ingredients in a saucepan except the egg. Let boil 10 minutes or *until celery and onions are tender*. Pour this mixture over the broken bread and toss. If it's not as moist as you like, add more turkey broth.

Add uncooked egg and mix lightly again.

Place dressing on greased cookie sheet and cook at 300° for 30 minutes. If you like it extremely moist, pile the dressing high. If you want drier dressing, spread it about two inches thick on your cookie sheet.

The new method for cooking dressing on a cookie sheet and not in the cavity of the bird is good for many reasons. The turkey can be easily sliced for freezing or sandwiches and it will have no sage flavor. Government bulletins also say there is a danger of bacteria in the body cavity of a stuffed turkey after it has been kept a few days.

This method also keeps your dressing from being "soggy" which it usually is when cooked five hours in a bird. When cooked on a cookie sheet it will be tender and crisp.

YOU'LL WANT A CHICKEN IN EVERY POT!

Are you tired of fried chicken and potatoes? Try this for a change:

Boil a hen . . . until it absolutely falls apart. But don't just boil the hen in plain water. Let me tell you what I found out!

Any time I boil an ol' hen, young hen, or just a hen—no matter how old she was—I boil it in "chicken stock base." (This is a condiment on the market which you will find in the spice department at your local grocery store.) I put at least one rounded teaspoon of chicken stock base into the water. This gives the chicken more flavor than you can imagine!

Your chicken can be boiled in the morning. After it literally falls apart, turn off the fire, remove the lid from the pot and let it cool. Place the chicken on a platter and remove all the meat from the bones.

Now here's what is going to make it so good:

Dip as much as you need of this rejuvenated broth from the stock that you have just cooked. Example: If you use packaged, *pre-cooked* rice as I do, dip one cup of this stock, putting it into another pan with one cup of water. Add a pinch of saffron and bring this to a boil. Then dump in two cups of rice, slam the lid on, twist the lid a little bit—this somehow seals the lid and prevents the moisture from escaping.

Put the chicken that you have stripped from its bones back into the remaining stock. Bring to a slow boil and make your gravy thickening. Into this thickening put another pinch of saffron. Within minutes this gravy will turn into a beautiful, golden-yellow, succulent dish. Too, this makes one old hen go a long way!

But here's where you are going to be most surprised. Just wait until you remove the top from that plain old rice! It will be brilliant yellow with a flavor all its own.

Often, I add chopped pimientos and chopped green peppers and celery to the rice. This gives it even more color. Or vary the rice from week to week by using chopped stuffed olives. This way you still have red and green, but the olives change the taste of the rice again, making an entirely new dish.

When putting the chicken and gravy into your serving dish, top it with fresh ground pepper.

Place serving of rice on plate, top with the chopped chicken in gravy and watch your family eat!

And ladies, the leftover chicken and gravy can be varied the next day by hard boiling some eggs . . . removing the yellow, chopping up the whites into little bite-size pieces and putting them into the gravy itself as you reheat it. Simply put a few pieces of bread in your toaster. Slice diagonally. Lay this on your plate, pour on some of that chicken and gravy which contains your chopped egg whites. Take the hard boiled yellow and, using your grater, grate the egg yolks on top of this open faced sandwich.

Serve with something red and something green, such as tomatoes and lettuce.

It's easy, quick, and delicious!

Look for a stewing chicken on sale. Pick up the saffron at the same time, and don't forget to buy a small bottle of chicken stock base.

STRETCH THAT BIRD!

Many people hesitate to buy turkeys or even roasting chickens except for Christmas, Thanksgiving, or other special days. Why? Turkey meat is plenty cheap! Chicken is cheap, too!

Go on and buy that turkey or hen. Roast it and eat the best part of it the first night.

The next night, serve sliced chicken or turkey sandwiches. *But,* save that broth and those drippings. After your family has gotten down to practically the carcass (that is, those bones and the dark meat), break the fowl apart and put in a pot of water, adding a little chicken bouillon, and let it boil for an hour or so.

The little bits of meat will literally fall off the bones. After boiling, set the pan aside and let it cool; then and only then start picking those bones. You will be amazed how much meat you will get from that old carcass!

This meat may either be thrown back into the broth and you can have chicken and dumplings that night, or you can make soup out of the broth and grind your chicken with the food chopper for a sandwich spread.

Always grind your meat first and while your chopper is still on the board get out those sweet pickles and run them through that grinder, too. The pickles will push out the leftover meat.

At the same time, if you happen to have a piece of celery in the kitchen, take your potato peeler and remove the strings from the celery. Run the stalk of celery through that grinder, too! Furthermore, do not throw away the leaves on the end of the stalk of celery. Grind them up, too! They're delicious.

All that is needed then is a dab of mayonnaise to make a delicious sandwich spread. After this is mixed, put it in a fruit jar and cap the top. This keeps it from drying out.

This mixture may be kept in your refrigerator and used not only for sandwiches but to stuff tomatoes. What a wonderful lunch for tired mothers! It makes a beautiful plate for supper, too. Serve on a lettuce leaf with a few crackers, pickled beets, carrot sticks, and maybe some green peas.

A BIRD IN THE HAND!

When scalding a chicken, add one teaspoon of soda to the boiling water. The feathers will come off easier and the flesh will be clean and white.

From New Mexico: "I tenderize chicken by rubbing the inside and outside with lemon juice before cooking."

From Vermont: "I don't continually baste large or small fowl when roasting.

"Using a pastry brush, I lather the bird with plain mayonnaise, getting under the wings and in the folds of the fowl. Then I sprinkle with garlic salt and pepper and roast as usual.

"You will have a nice brown crispy crust on the bird. This works equally well for baking the small broiler halves of chicken."

Next time you truss up a turkey, try using big sharp safety pins! They are quick and easy to use and you can put them exactly where you need them. You'll never go back to needles, string and skewers.

RICE TO THE OCCASION!

I receive many requests for recipes for casseroles and meat substitutes that are not in the ordinary cook books, and I have found one that is up on Cloud Nine.

It is called rice soufflé.

Here 'tis.

1 cup cold cooked rice	2 tablespoons butter
3 eggs separated	½ cup milk
¼ pound grated Cheddar cheese	pinch of salt

Separate the whites of three eggs from their yolks. Beat the whites until stiff.

Add the yolks to one cup of cold cooked rice. (This may be leftover rice or cooked minute rice.)

Blend in one-half cup of milk, two tablespoons of butter, and one-fourth pound of grated Cheddar cheese. Stir all of these well.

Gently fold in the beaten egg whites, adding a little salt to taste, and bake in a greased casserole in a slow oven for about one-half hour to 45 minutes at 300° *or* until the soufflé is brown on top.

Now here's what I did for variation and to please the Rock of Gibraltar (that's the man I have been living with all these years). He likes hot tuna fish and happens to be the only one in the family who does. So . . . to please the Old Rock, I pour half of the soufflé into my casserole after taking a piece of foil and lining half of it, leaving a bit of the foil turned up to divide the soufflé into two parts.

With the other half of the soufflé already mixed, and before pouring it into the foil-lined portion of my casserole, I add a half-can of chunk tuna (or canned shrimp) after draining it thoroughly of the oil. (The soufflé may be divided and cooked in two separate casseroles *or* individual serving dishes.)

This little trick left me with two completely separate dishes, a happy husband, and all members of the family pleased!

Ladies, this is an economical dish and a wonderful meat substitute. It is perfectly beautiful when it comes to the table; its light, it's fluffy, and it's tasty! Try it.

When cooking rice, add a spoonful of vinegar or the same amount of lemon juice, and it will be light, separated, and fluffy.

When rice has burned, place a piece of fresh white bread crust—you can use the heel—on top of the rice and cover the pot again. Within a few minutes the scorched taste will disappear. Later just remove the bread.

For bridal favors try tinted, *scented* rice! This makes a lovely favor for showers and it is simple to make. After tinting uncooked rice with food dye, allow to dry. Add a few drops of cologne and a few small artificial flowers. Place in tulle or net and tie with a ribbon.

GIVE FISH A LEMON BATH

From Montana: "My family loves fried fish but they don't like the fish odor that seems to last for days. Now I soak the fish in lemon juice for about 20 to 25 minutes, roll in meal, fry in deep fat—no odor."

From Kansas: "In the preparation of shrimp, never boil them. First, remove the shell and de-vein if desired. Then place the peeled shrimp into a pan with a tight lid. Add salt.

"Have a kettle of boiling hot water ready. Pour over shrimp and stir a second. Clamp tight lid on top and after a few minutes they will be done to perfection. Never tough or tasteless from being boiled too long.

"The size of shrimp will determine the time used for completing the process. For instance, small or average-size shrimp take about four minutes. The large ones require about six minutes.

"You may take one out to test for your personal liking. Do not place the pan on heat. I usually place mine in my sink. Then I allow the shrimp to drain.

"When dry, place in a covered jar and they will keep for a week in the refrigerator, where they are always ready for any emergency."

From Oklahoma: "I clean my shrimp by running an ice pick down the back toward their tails. The shell and vein pull off easily. Try it! I like it better than a de-veiner."

5.

Do-It-Yourself, Kid!

━━━━━━━━━━━━━━━━━━━━━━━━━━━━━━━━━━━━━━━

WASH-'N'-WEAR APRON

For women who wear aprons . . . it is utterly ridiculous for us to make them out of cotton that has to be washed, starched and ironed weekly!

Take your favorite apron for a pattern and make one out of an old bath towel.

When your hands are wet, just wipe them on the apron but—best of all—you can throw it in the laundry once or twice a week and wear it again with no ironing required.

MAKE YOUR OWN SHADES

You can make your own kitchen window shades out of table oilcloth.

Buy the proper length and color to match your kitchen decor. Just remove the old shade from the roller, and tack the new oilcloth back on the same roller.

These shades can be washed when they get soiled, or

can be wiped with a cloth. They look nice in the bath-room, too.

NAPKIN BECOMES HANDY BAG

To make use of napkins left over from a set, make bags out of them by sewing two napkins together . . . then either make a drawstring top, or sew one of them into a wire coat hanger.

You will find many uses for these. You can use one made of larger napkins to hold filled stamp books, smaller ones for jar rings and small plastic bags, etc.

SPRUCE UP KITCHEN CHAIRS

You can cover kitchen or breakfast room chairs with looped, shag rugs that can be bought on sale. They are wonderful and so rich looking!

Everyone comments on them. The covers don't show dust, grease spots, soil or "seat" prints. These covers can be removed from the chairs and washed in your washing machine. I thumb-tacked mine on the bottom of the removable seat boards on my dining room chairs.

It's easy, simple, and gives you a sense of accomplishment to be able to have something so fabulous in your kitchen, dining, or breakfast room.

And if I may make one more suggestion . . . think about using terry bath mats for this same purpose (provided you can get some matching ones on sale).

Bath mats are easy to tack on the chair, cheap, no trouble to wash, and give an entirely different effect. They come in such beautiful colors and textures and are just about the right size.

TABLECLOTH TRICKS

For those who have a table in the kitchen and do not like changing tablecloths every day or so which have to be washed and ironed . . . make your own from terry cloth!

These can be thrown in the washing machine, require no ironing, and spots come right out.

If you need a nice durable, easy to clean, non-slip tablecloth—try plastic upholstery. Sure is wonderful.

This upholstery comes in 64-inch widths and you can purchase whatever length you wish. It comes in pretty patterns, too. It's especially good when there are little children around the house, for there always seems to be at least one spill at every meal. Sure is easy to wipe off with a sponge.

For a kitchen tablecloth you can look in the drapery department of department stores and find the nicest designs from remnants!

Most of these come 54 inches or more wide. Make a one inch hem around the remnant. This material is heavy and a much better grade than most of us can afford to buy for the kitchen table!

For those who have picnic tables outside and do not like to use oilcloth but yet hesitate to use their nice tablecloths . . . you can buy an odd shower curtain on sale and simply use pinking shears to snip off all the edges. If it is too long you can use what is left over to line bathroom shelves.

From Tennessee: "Every year we have a smorgasbord dinner at our church. Our aim is to make money, not spend it.

"We serve several hundred dinners and use place mats for each dinner served.

"This year I went to a wallpaper store and asked for leftover rolls of paper. The owner handed me a sample book of last year's styles.

"I removed the sheets from the book, cut each sheet into two parts and edged each piece with pinking shears. They made such beautiful place mats that my daughters and I saved some of them to use when our card clubs meet."

For those who cannot get outdated books of wallpaper samples . . . did you know that wallpaper stores have what they call "broken rolls"?

These are sold at bargain rates. Buy a broken roll, even though you are not going to make place mats. This is wonderful to line shelves, drawers, wrap packages, and for many other things around the house.

Don't throw away those old worn out tablecloths with holes in them. Take your pinking shears and cut them in small sizes to be used later as dish towels, hand towels, etc.

By using your pinking shears, this will save hemming each towel. Good tablecloths, such as linen, shouldn't ravel. As the center part is usually worn, cut these cloths from the edges.

PRETTY UP THE DISH-WASHING DEPARTMENT

Husbands' old shirts make the most wonderful dish-towels imaginable and they have absolutely no lint.

The center back is much too nice to use for ordinary rags. So pink the edges with shears and use the backs for dishtowels. They have been washed so often that they are nice and soft. And the colored shirts will look so pretty hanging in the kitchen.

Buy a half yard of plain nylon net . . . yes, the kind with which you ordinarily make evening dresses . . . for the most marvelous dishcloths. You can buy this in colors or in white (whatever appeals to you to go with your kitchen decor).

This comes 72 inches wide, so by taking your scissors and cutting it in four pieces you will have four 18 x 18 inch dishcloths for your kitchen. These do not have to be hemmed as they do not ravel.

We have found these excellent for scrubbing pots which have "goop" in them such as mashed potatoes, rice, etc., which ordinarily make a mess out of our daily dishrag. This cloth will not mildew, mold, or smell.

From New York: "In one- or two-person families where there are very few dishes, it is a nuisance and a waste to

69

use the dishpan and soap powders for every cup or luncheon dish.

"We make soap bags. We crochet them of store-string or cut up old dishcloths and sew them so they are about four and one-half by two and one-half inches. Leave a hole in one end.

"Cut off a piece of soap and slide in the opening.

"This soap bag is always soapy, always handy, and it is not, as might be supposed, wasteful of the soap. We couldn't live without it. It does not get sour or need washing out as a dishcloth usually does."

6.

Mealtime Memos

▀▀

THE VERSATILE POTATO

In most families, potatoes are the "backbone" of the main meal. There are so many delicious ways to serve them. Here are a few:

From a restaurant manager: "One thing we never do is peel potatoes with any kind of knife except stainless steel.

"When placing potatoes in the water for boiling, I feel quite qualified to suggest that housewives add one teaspoon of vinegar or a teaspoon of fresh lemon juice to the water in which they boil their potatoes. This will make potatoes snowy white.

"I find the most amazing thing about running restaurants is this: housewives who must cook potatoes every day at home in order to make the budgets stretch always order mashed potatoes when they go to a restaurant! I think the reason is because the potatoes are always white and fluffy. One reason for the fluffiness is that we use electric beaters and instead of milk—which the average housewife usually pours into her pot—we use water and lots of butter."

From Connecticut: "When we make our mashed potatoes, we use a pressure cooker. It takes only eight minutes to cook potatoes in ours. Do *not* drain off the water before mashing. We use an electric beater, add margarine, and dried, skim milk. Our potatoes are always fluffy and white! Be sure to follow the directions for your particular type of pressure cooker. They take very little water."

Here's a use for leftover mashed potatoes: Boil only enough new potatoes so that the fresh ones and the left-over ones will be enough for your meal.

When the potatoes that you are boiling are done, but not soft, and the water has almost boiled away, add the leftover potatoes to the boiling ones . . . just long enough to heat through!

Drain and mash as usual. You would never guess there were any leftovers being served!

From Michigan: "When my husband or guests are late for dinner and my mashed potatoes are ready to be served, I just drain the water off of them (mash if you desire), then place a cotton or linen napkin over them and put the cover back on top of the pot.

"This way they will remain hot for at least another one-half hour or more."

From Kentucky: "I reheat my leftover mashed potatoes by putting them in the top of a double boiler. I cook them from 20 to 30 minutes. Then I just rewhip them. They are just as nice as fresh-cooked potatoes."

Potatoes will mash without flying out of the bowl if you will cut them in small pieces before cooking!

If you have trouble with liquids splashing from your electric mixer when whipping things, throw a clean dish-towel over the entire mixer! Your walls or drainboard won't get spattered!

TOP-OF-THE-STOVE BAKED POTATOES

This tip came from a woman with young children:
"I take three or four medium-size potatoes and wrap

them in a piece of aluminum foil. I lay this package evenly on a gas stove burner and turn it to the lowest possible heat. After a while, I turn the entire package over on the other side. I test this with a fork for doneness. I find I can have baked potatoes without muss or fuss, and in less time than it takes in the oven."

To me this was unbelievable! Then I tried it. . . .

Many mothers with children cook baked potatoes, but equally important is that these mothers would bake themselves a potato this way for their midday snack (which they don't often take time out to prepare because it is too much trouble), if they only knew how easy this method is.

I baked three potatoes this top-of-the-stove way. Instead of putting them all in one foil container, however, I tried different methods. I put holes in one potato by running an ice pick completely through the potato. I wrapped this in one sheet of foil. Another potato was wrapped in about three pieces of foil, but this one I greased first.

The potatoes were absolutely delicious—and there was no dirty pan to wash!

When potatoes are cooked on top of the stove in the above manner, you can take a knife and slit through the foil to add butter and leave the potatoes in the foil-covered jackets. This makes a mighty pretty "something new" on that ordinary supper plate!

For those who cannot eat butter and oleo, the juice from a fresh lemon suffices on nearly anything that these two items are used for. Fresh lemon juice when squeezed on a baked potato is out of this world! So is chicken or beef bouillon.

Have you ever wanted *one* baked potato, and hated to heat the oven?

A coffee can with an old jar lid inside for the potato

to rest on . . . is perfect! Cover this and place on the lowest flame possible on the top burner of your stove and in 20 minutes, you have a perfect baked potato!

When baking potatoes . . . for those who love to eat the skins and want them real crisp . . . use bacon grease.

Prevent soil in your oven by placing the baked potato on a tiny piece of foil when placing it on the oven rack.

The baking of potatoes won't hold up supper if you cut a thin slice from each end and made an incision in its sides. You will be surprised how much faster they will bake.

Did you ever wish you could bake potatoes in only 13 minutes?

You can, and you don't even have to heat the oven. Wrap the potatoes in foil, place them on a rack in your pressure cooker and add water up to the rack. Cook 10 to 15 minutes, depending upon the size. When done, they taste like regular oven-baked potatoes.

THREE-IN-ONE

From Pennsylvania: "When boiling potatoes, I always cook three times the amount needed.

"I mash one-third for the immediate meal. I cut one-third of the batch in pieces for potato salad, and mash the last third and shape them into potato patties!

"I find that I can make three dishes in the same time it usually takes to make one. The potatoes for the salad can be refrigerated and the patties frozen! Only one dirty pan and meals for three days."

Some people don't peel their potatoes before boiling them for potato salad. They say the best part of the potato is just under the skin. In this case, while the potatoes are still warm, use a paring knife and skin each potato. This saves much of the potato that would ordinarily be thrown away. Then cut potatoes into pieces.

Incidentally, when boiling unpeeled potatoes for potato salad, cook your eggs in the same pan with your potatoes. Place eggs on top of the potatoes. Both foods are cooked at the same time and there is only one pan to wash!

If the condiments (whatever you use) are mixed with the potatoes while they are still warm, the potatoes absorb the flavors better. I mix mayonnaise, vinegar, celery salt, savory salt, mustard, chopped pimiento, salt and pepper, etc., together before pouring over the warm potatoes. Mix well. *Then* add chopped eggs and sliced stuffed olives.

A little dash of mustard added to potato salad is what gives it the beautiful golden color and the illusion that twice as many eggs have been used. It gives a tart taste, too. This is a trick which many good restaurants use.

This is a beautiful salad when dipped by spoonful on a lettuce leaf and topped with a dab of mayonnaise and some paprika.

You know what a mess boiled-over potatoes or any starchy food is on your stove.

You can prevent this by putting a small pat of butter in the water. You can then fill up the pan more, without it boiling over. Leave the lid slightly ajar.

Keeping potatoes in your refrigerator will eliminate the growth of "eyes" and also keep them from becoming pithy.

NO STRINGS

If you are using cooked pumpkin or sweet potatoes and see that they are going to be "stringy," cheer up. Put them in a large bowl and use your electric mixer at high speed and beat for a few seconds, then reduce the speed to low.

Disconnect the beater and hold it over the sink, and spray rinse it. You will be amazed at how many strings are on those beaters! Repeat the beating process again. This gets your potatoes and pumpkin smooth as butter.

AS ONE CABBAGE SLAW FAN TO ANOTHER

For those of you who just must have your cabbage slaw—and I am one of you—let me give you a top secret that will make it really different.

About once a month I go to an out-of-the-way drugstore to eat. I walked into one recently and had the "blue plate luncheon." It cost 85¢. Not only did I lick the platter clean, but walked out with an $85,000 hint! Cabbage slaw . . . this was the best cabbage slaw that I ever tasted. Color probably had lots to do with it.

Here's how it is made:

Cut the cabbage in two with a stainless steel butcher knife. Soak the half-heads in salty ice water for about one hour. (Gals, I found out that this makes it so crisp it actually crunches between your teeth.)

After removing the cabbage, shake off the excess water. Cut the half-cabbage in half again. Now you are left with one-fourth of a head of cabbage. Place this on your cutting board. Take your sharpest knife (ladies, if it isn't sharp, for goodness' sake take care of that little matter right now) and, placing one of the cut sides of the head of the cabbage down on your cutting board, shred it as thinly as possible so that the cabbage will end up in teeny shreds. As the cabbage will have become so cold from the soaking it will be easier to slice.

Now, cabbage slaw is cabbage slaw. However, here's what makes this cabbage slaw different:

Take boiled eggs which you have dropped in beet juice and now won't be white but a gorgeous purple color—and grate on the biggest part of your grater. Throw this dyed egg into your cabbage slaw! Then put your dressing on.

And I also got the secret of this delicious dressing. Tartness is one of the things which we do not often find in dressings. You may use any dressing you wish in cabbage slaw. However, here is the recipe that came from the cook at the drugstore:

2 ounces of oil—any kind of cooking oil	¼ teaspoon celery salt
	1 ounce mayonnaise
1 ounce of lime or lemon juice	salt and fresh ground
½ teaspoon prepared mustard	pepper to taste
a dash of paprika	

Mix this together, pour over the slaw and put back into the refrigerator. When you can't stand it another minute, eat it and drool!

DRY-'EM-YOURSELF CELERY TOPS

I would like to tell you about celery tops and what I learned recently about them.

A few months ago a woman wrote about the waste we have in our kitchens. One of the many things she mentioned was how we women cut off celery tops and throw them away, and later buy them in a box at the store. She pointed out how valuable they were when it came to vitamins and how many ways we could use them.

For instance, celery tops are wonderful when chopped up fresh and added to lettuce salad.

She gave me a hint as to how to preserve them. Here's how:

When you buy stalk celery, wash it thoroughly. Put it on a dough or cutting board, take a sharp knife and cut the tops off. I found that if you start at the end and cut the celery leaves off every one-fourth inch . . . they end up beautifully.

Now once in awhile you will get a piece of celery stalk itself in here. Never mind. Leave it. It's wonderful later when you get ready to use the dried celery for other things.

Take a cookie sheet and cover it with a piece of foil. Put all the celery leaves on the covered cookie sheet. There will be so many that you will wonder where you are going to put them. Take it from me . . . in the next few days there will be practically nothing.

Put this cookie tin in your oven. If you have a gas stove the pilot light alone will dry the leaves out in a few days. If you have an electric stove . . . *after* you get through using the oven every time, let it cool a bit and while still warm place these celery tops back on the rack in your oven.

Once the leaves start dehydrating, fold the foil around them to make a bag. Keep this in the oven until *all* moisture is gone.

In time (a few days) the leaves will shrink to practically nothing. Then take your hands and crush the leaves and particles of celery stems. Put in jars and cap well.

Next time you make soup, those nice boiled new potatoes, etc., crush in some of these dried celery leaves. I even put them in spaghetti sauce and it's delicious!

Save any way you can, gals, and never throw away anything that can be utilized. And I have learned that when celery is cheap and on sale—watch your ads in the papers—you can buy two stalks of celery and get twice as much for your money. Saves work when drying celery leaves, too.

LETTUCE TALK

When separating head lettuce for use on sandwiches, etc., hold the head firmly cupped in hand with the stem down.

Hit the stem end sharply against a cutting board or the edge of your sink. The entire core of the lettuce will lift right out with just a twist of the wrist.

Run cold water from the faucet in this little hole and all the leaves will separate beautifully.

Did you know that you could take a piece of waxed paper and sprinkle paprika on it and roll the cut side of a damp head of lettuce in this and it will make the prettiest red lettuce you ever saw?

Gives color to plain lettuce when you are out of tomatoes.

To keep lettuce fresh a long time, wrap in a damp cloth and then put into a plastic bag in the refrigerator.

Salt wilts lettuce in a short time and makes it tough. Consequently, salt should not be used on a lettuce salad until immediately before the salad is served.

SPIN-DRY THOSE SALAD GREENS

Did you ever hear of drying salad greens (lettuce, watercress, etc.) in your washing machine?

It sounds crazy, but try it, it's wonderful! Wash the greens well, shake out as much water as you can and place them in small heaps in a clean dishtowel or clean pillow case (about one head per towel). Fold the ends across loosely, place in the washer and set the control for the final "spin-dry" cycle.

The greens do not get mangled and they will stay in the towel. They come out nice and dry and may be stored in a plastic freezer canister. They will keep for a week this way in the refrigerator, and will always be ready for salads.

This is especially useful to women who make salads for large parties and church suppers.

From Honolulu: "When I buy salad greens, I wash them and separate them into the amounts I ordinarily use to make our daily salads.

"I then put *each* portion into a plastic bag and re-frigerate them. These individual portions are always crisp and ready to use and one does not have any greens left to be put back in the refrigerator. Saves time."

From New Mexico: "I tear—never cut—salad greens and after washing gently, place them in a large salad bowl on a layer of damp paper toweling. I cover the greens with a double layer of *dry* paper toweling upon which I have placed six to eight ice cubes. I then set aside in the coldest part of the refrigerator for at least one hour.

"When ready to use, the greens are crisp and crunchy. The paper towels catch most of the ice water."

From New Jersey: "When making any kind of salad that calls for pickles, hard boiled eggs, celery, onions, green peppers and so forth, I use the coarse side of my grater. This is the side with the big holes. I find it much faster and easier and it makes a very neat salad."

From Rhode Island: "I just found a real tricky way of saving. I suppose that over half of the families in the United States have lettuce and tomato salad at least three times a week.

"I have been married for 20 years and I don't think I can remember when I didn't make too much or too little salad.

"Everyone knows that this type of salad is no good when left over. I have discovered how to save it. The secret is—don't put dressing on your lettuce and tomatoes. Put oil dressings and condiments on the table and let each person season his own salad.

"The salad that is left over may be put in a glass bowl and placed in the refrigerator and covered with a damp cloth or paper towel. But the most surprising part of it all is . . . how good it tastes the next day when chores are piled high to the ceiling and there isn't time to cook lunch.

"Then it is time to grab that fresh lettuce, pour your dressing on it, get out a few crackers, a big glass of skim milk, and enjoy your low calorie diet."

PRETTY UP THE CUCUMBERS

After peeling a cucumber, take a fork and scrape the sides from top-to-bottom. Scrape down hard. Then slice your cucumber. This will leave a little design around each slice. So pretty and easy.

Soak cucumbers in salt and water an hour before using. They are more digestible.

NO MORE TEARS!

A little hint that I tested is putting onions in the refrigerator, and leaving them for a few days . . . then cutting them to see if they smell, or caused me to cry.

Don't think that this is a screwy idea, because it absolutely is not! Two days later I cut the onions half-in-two with a knife, and tested them. No one in my family could smell any onion odor on the cut onion!

Then I decided to cut them up fine—such as when I make spaghetti, etc., and see if they smelled. Do you know that none of us had tears, nor could any of us smell any odor? Keep a few onions in your refrig for daily use.

However, I have decided that there is no need to overload the refrigerator with a whole bag of onions. Why? Because we do not use a whole bag of onions at one time.

When you buy a bag of onions, put them in your cupboard. But take two onions and store them on one of the shelves of your refrigerator. Then, when you get ready to cut onions for that hamburger or spaghetti, use the cold onions.

When you take these two onions from your refrigerator to use in whatever you are preparing . . . grab another onion or two from under your counter and put back into your refrigerator.

Another hint is: When you need only a small amount of onion . . . peel the onion as you would an orange. Peel off as much of the onion as you need. Wrap the rest of it in wax paper and put back in the refrigerator.

An empty plastic cottage cheese carton works beautifully for storing cut onions or partially used onions in your refrigerator.

From New York: "When I grate onions, I always leave the 'head' on one end and use it as a handle. This way I save my fingernails."

"When onion is grated down near to the end . . . just discard the rest. No waste really, because this part is usually cut off and thrown away."

From Denver: "When making spaghetti sauce . . . instead of using onions, use a package of onion soup! This gives the sauce a nice flavor."

From Utah: "My family does not liked chopped or grated onions in anything. So I hit upon the idea of making my own fresh onion juice.

"Take an onion but do *not* remove the outside skin. Cut the onion in half with a knife. Then just use your dime-store squeezer and squeeze it as if it were an orange or lemon.

"The results: heavenly fresh onion juice! This can be used in anything you are cooking."

From Honolulu: "I cut green onion tops *very* fine with my kitchen shears and freeze them. I always have them ready for dips and so forth. They serve as chives when chives are not available."

Stale, dried-up cheese turns into a delicious spread when placed into the meat grinder with a few chunks of raw onion.

STORING FRESH PARSLEY

To keep parsley crisp and fresh, place bunch upright in a wide-mouthed jar with an airtight lid. Put just enough water in the jar to cover the stems without it touching the leaves. Store in refrigerator.

You can remove as much as you need at a time, but always be sure to replace the lid and keep the water level below the leaves.

Never use a can of dry parsley without testing first to see if it has bugs in it. Always pour some out in a saucer to test it before using.

WILD, BUT IT WORKS!

Frozen peas can be shelled very fast with a wringer-type washer. Put a pan on one side of the wringer to catch the peas and the pods go on through. You will think peas will go through the wringer and be mashed the moment the pod hits the wringer, but they will pop out *before* they go through. A very fast job can be done this way.

VEGETABLE SNACKS

From Florida: "For in-between snacks I clean radishes, celery, peppers, etc., spear them with a toothpick, and put them in my refrigerator so that one can have a snack, with no effort."

To peel a tomato, spear it on a fork, hold it over the gas flame, and turn it gently until the skin softens. Rinse under cold water, and the skin comes right off!

If you ever have a little tomato paste left over from cooking . . . place it in a small container and pour vegetable oil over the top of the tomato paste before putting it into the refrigerator and it will keep for weeks, without molding. When ready to use the paste again, just pour the oil off.

ARE YOU A BEAN-STRINGER?

From Kansas: "I know there are many people who *string* beans!

"I am a farmer's wife and I have found that after the beans are washed you can plunge them into boiling water for about three minutes and then drain. The strings then can be removed with complete ease."

From New Jersey: "Instead of the agonizing chore of stringing beans (the pole bean variety), my husband suggested that I use my potato peeler.

"I break off each end of the bean and then peel the two sides where the strings are with the potato peeler. This might seem to waste some of the bean, but it sure beats having to string your beans by hand.

"Using this method . . . your beans are absolutely stringless."

From Montreal: "When pouring hot water from vegetables, I always have the cold water running in the sink. This stops the steam from hurting or scalding my hands."

Ever use an egg slicer to slice raw mushrooms to sauté? It's sure, quick, and uniform.

We cook many things in double boilers. Utilize the heat when using the bottom part. If you have boiled potatoes or carrots in the bottom, wait until they are nearly done and then put peas (they only need to be heated) in the top part. Slap on the lid and use that burner to kill two birds at the same time. Saves heat and you only have to wash one lid. Also, while cooking carrots in the bottom part, you can make cream sauce in the top. Pour the sauce into the carrots. Saves time and heat.

Do you ever put frozen vegetables such as peas on to cook and worry that the peas in the center of the frozen lump won't get cooked without overcooking the loose peas?

Well, before opening the package . . . whack it! Whack all four sides. Then, take hold of the opposite end and whack all four sides again. I whack them hard on my kitchen counter.

If you are recklessly violent you will find when you open a package that each pea is separate and ready to be cooked evenly.

FRESHEN UP CANNED VEGETABLES

From Georgia: "I make canned and frozen vegetables taste like those grandmother used to make and nearly as good as the fresh ones we used to pick out of our garden, if I grate a quarter of a small onion and add it and a dash of sugar and salt to the water in which I boil all frozen and canned vegetables.

"I let the water and the condiments boil until the onion is well-cooked. Then put my frozen or canned vegetables in.

"To get back to the old-fashioned cookin', did you know that when you use salt in vegetables, you should also use a pinch of sugar, too?

"When I use canned tomatoes, I always—depending on the size of the can of tomatoes—add at least a level teaspoon of sugar to them as I find it cuts the acid taste of the canned tomatoes! This is the answer to good eatin'."

From Hollywood: "Whenever I am using canned vegetables and the oven is on, I open the can of vegetables, and remove the label (*this* is most important!) and place the can on the floor of the oven.

"After 15 minutes, the can of vegetables is hot. I remove it and put it right into my serving dish. Out into the garbage goes that tin can! No pot to wash and dry, and no extra fuel cost!"

BEATS PEELING BEETS

From Indiana: "Recently I saw my neighbor peeling fresh beets with a paring knife and wondered if there are others who haven't learned the easy way to peel beets.

"Place the beets in a pan of water, leave one-half inch of the stem and the root of the beet *on*. This keeps the sand out of the beet while cooking! Bring the water to a boil and continue to boil for about 15 minutes.

"Remove the beets from the fire and place them under cold water in the sink. Allow the water to run on the beets until they are cool enough to handle.

"Then cut off both ends of the beet and the peeling will slip right off. Slice, dice, or leave whole and place in clean pan of water—which will have *no* sand at all—and cook until done."

NO MORE "BULLETS"

A bean cooker from Kentucky wrote the following:
"It surprises me how anyone can complain that they

cannot soak, boil, or pressure cook dry beans and make them tender.

"Do not add the salt to dry beans until the beans are already tender, or you may *still* have 'bullets' after hours of cooking.

"Even strongly salted seasoning-meat will have somewhat the same effect. For additionally improved texture of the bean, a *small* pinch of baking soda will help prevent skin-cracking and consequent mushiness."

I have been cooking beans for years. I absolutely couldn't believe this, so I tried it. I took two identical pans and two separate cups of navy (pea beans) beans and divided the water equally in each pan. I put the beans on burners side by side and cooked them at the same temperature. I added salt to one and cooked the other plain. You should have seen the difference!

The beans which I loaded with salt were hard as rocks and a yellow color and later the skins started coming off.

The unsalted beans became white and soft sooner and were beautiful. They can be salted after cooking.

Next time you cook beans . . . test this yourself and see. You will never believe it until you do.

FREEZE LEFTOVER PIMIENTOS

From Boston: "One of my pet saving methods is for canned pimientos.

"Whenever I open a can of pimientos, I wrap them separately in aluminum foil and replace them in the can. I cover the top of the can and put them in the freezer until I am ready to use pimiento again.

"When frozen, these little individual pimientos can be shaved off in fine slivers. This beats having them spoil in the refrigerator after having been left open a few days."

SAND-FREE STRAWBERRIES

Strawberries are really summertime ambrosia. They are expensive and not something which we set on our table every day. Therefore . . . I gave this much thought and experimentation.

I found the best way to wash strawberries which were to be eaten immediately was to wash them first while the stem and "greenery" were still attached to the strawberry itself. I found that if they were first washed to remove sand, while the stem was still connected, the juice did not run out. Nor were many grains of sand redeposited in the cut ends.

Strawberries must be washed well. The little seeds seem to hold the soil. The best way to do the job is to float them in a pan of water!

Do not put them in a dry pan and run water on them as this bruises the strawberries. Fill your pan half full of water, dump the strawberries in and then toss them lightly with your fingers. Then put the pan under your *cold* water faucet (a spray type gadget is the best) and let them tumble themselves. We found that this gets most of the sand off.

Once you see sand in the bottom of this pan, turn the water faucet off. Have another pan set aside which is also half-filled with water. Take your fingers and gently lift the strawberries, which are floating on top of the water by this time, and place them in the second pan.

Keep doing this until there is no residue of dirt or sand at the bottom of the water. Then remove the "greenery" from the strawberries and re-wash gently.

Place one layer of berries on the bottom of a glass bowl and *lightly* sprinkle them with sugar. Place another layer or two on top of this and sprinkle it a little heavier with sugar. When you put the last batch in, sprinkle it the heaviest with sugar. The sugar drips from the top layer of strawberries and falls down over the two layers on the bottom. Set the bowl of strawberries into the refrigerator to chill.

NYLON NET LEMON STRAINER

I was invited to an elegant restaurant recently for dinner.

I have often wondered why people pay exorbitant prices for food. Now I know. It's because they get service and unique ideas which other restaurants do not offer.

This idea concerns lemons.

The lemons served with our tomato juice and salad were cut in half—crosswise—and wrapped with a piece of plain old cheesecloth! The cheesecloth looked mighty strange in the expensive setting, but it kept the juice from squirting across the room and the seeds from falling in our food.

When I came home, I cut a lemon in half and tried the cheesecloth. It's O.K. but I thought of something even better. You know what? Nylon net!

Try green or yellow nylon net. The green reminds you of a lime, adds color to your tables and matches the lettuce. The yellow is ever so delightful, because it enhances the color of the lemon itself.

I cut a lemon in half and wrapped it in my nylon net, placing the cut part of the lemon on my little square of nylon net. I gathered it on top and twisted it slightly, tying it with a piece of wire from some vegetables.

I serve this on our table just as the elegant restaurants do. You put it on a plate, face down. Each one passes the plate along and squeezes out as much lemon as he needs for iced tea, fish, salad, and so forth . . . and places it back in the dish face down again. The net prevents the seeds and pulp from getting into your food.

When your dinner is over, all you have to do is put the whole saucer which contains the sliced lemon back into your refrigerator (in case you have not used all of the good part of that lemon) and it can be reused the following meal. This saves lemons, too.

Another good thing about the nylon net is that it does not absorb the juices from the lemon as the cotton cloth does which that restaurant used!

A woman from Arkansas told me that a lemon heated before the juice is extracted will produce almost twice as much juice as a cold one. This idea really seems crazy, but it is absolutely true. I tried this hint and found it so satisfactory that now everytime I cook fish sticks or anything in the oven which requires fresh lemon juice, a few minutes before the food is done, I always place my lemons in the oven and heat them for a few minutes.

Here's a tip from a chef: Lemons with the smoothest skin and the least points on each end are by far better flavored and have more juice than rough-skinned, elongated ones.

PUT BANANAS IN REFRIGERATOR, BUT . . .

From Connecticut: "Bananas will keep when refrigerated in a tightly closed jar. This is especially useful when feeding small babies.

"Do not peel the banana, but cut off the amount you want to use. The unused portion will keep several days without turning dark if kept in a tightly closed jar."

From Maryland: "I slice my bananas with a silver knife and they do not turn dark."

If you want something different for breakfast, slice a banana lengthwise . . . leaving it in the skin. Sprinkle with salt, sugar, or lemon juice. Place on the plate and serve it for breakfast. Eat it with a spoon!

When serving a half grapefruit, if you will cut a thin slice off the bottom, if will rest more securely on the plate and not topple.

Did you ever put cranberries through a food chopper when making cranberry salad. What a mess!

There will be no more clogging of the chopper or too much juice if you freeze the berries first and grind them while they are still frozen.

From Delaware: "Several hours before it's time to pack my husband's lunch, I put canned fruit into a plastic container and set it in my freezer.

"When I fix his lunch, I put his sandwich on top of the fruit. It keeps the rest of the lunch cool and the fruit is thawed by the time he is ready to eat it."

When using fruit cocktail in gelatin desserts . . . save the cherries out of the fruit to doll up the salad later!

7.

Be a Washday Winner

━━━━━━━━━━━━━━━━━━━━━━━━━━━━━━━━━━━━━━━

TRY VINEGAR RINSE IF YOU'RE IN THE DARK

A woman asked me how to wash dark cotton dresses and not have them come out looking as if they had been floured. Hers were full of white streaks and when she ironed them they looked even worse.

I told her to use a detergent (a neutral detergent is best) and be sure that the clothes are rinsed well!

I swear by that good old household product . . . vinegar! I rinse all dark things—including husband's socks—in a solution of vinegar water. Use at least a half-cup of vinegar in the rinse water.

I do not rinse this vinegar water out! The odor will leave when it is dry and it also (in my opinion) reduces body odors.

If your garment has much soap film, it may take more than one washing to remove it.

You should also use spray starch on the *wrong* side of the garment. Iron on the *wrong* side too.

MAKE A LINT-CATCHER FOR WASHER

A friend recently had a huge plumbing bill because the main disposal pipes in her house were blocked solid with lint from the washing machine.

One of her friends suggested using an old nylon stocking slipped over the drain hose so that *just* the foot was hanging free. The leg part of the stocking was anchored by tying or using a tight elastic band slipped over the end of the drain hose to secure it in place.

I tried this myself and the results were amazing. In just four days a ball of lint the size of my fist had accumulated in the foot of the stocking itself.

From Connecticut: "I used plastic screen to make a 'sock' or 'little bag' for the end of my washing machine hose to filter the dirty water as it spins out! I simply cut the desired amount of plastic screen needed (about 12 inches long and 6 inches wide) and sewed it on my sewing machine, leaving one end open in the bag, of course. Then I clamped it on and presto, no more lint problem!

"I can easily see when my little plastic bag is full and needs to be emptied! Then it's a simple matter to turn the 'sock' inside out, remove the lint, turn it again and recap it on the hose."

NATURE'S BLEACH

Rather than use chemical bleach on your dish towels to whiten them, spread them on the grass in the sun instead of hanging them on the clothesline. They will be snowy white.

While traveling through Mexico, I happened to notice that all of the Mexicans who were "in the laundry business" laid their clothes on the green grass. After asking a few of them why, our answer was that the "green" in the grass is what bleaches the sheets, pillow cases, and bath towels.

I also found out that when women get a dingy load of laundry they leave the sheets, shirts, etc., on the green grass overnight. They claim that the dew which falls at night and the sunshine the next morning do all the work. I cannot contest this even though all home economists do not agree.

After all, you don't have anything to lose. You have used no bleach, no extra soap or energy. In case you just happen to have a few articles in your house which need whitening, try it.

TEST FOR BLEACH CONTENT

One woman asked me how to determine whether a detergent has bleach in it.

The National Institute of Rug Cleaning says that one method that might be used is to take ink, such as a *washable* blue-black, put it in a glass and add lots of water to it. Then, if you add some of the detergent which you think has a bleach, it most likely will remove the color.

Here's how to tell the difference between a neutral "non-built" detergent and a "built" detergent.

Wet your hands and pick up some of the dry detergent. If some of the detergent dissolves and the alkali causes the hands to become warm, this means the detergent is "built."

Do not pour undiluted liquid bleach into your washing machine. Dilute one-half cup of bleach with a quart of water and then pour it into the machine.

It is better to add the bleach after the laundry has been washing a few minutes.

The suds have then saturated the fabric and this gives the bleach a chance to do its own magic work.

One simple thing that can save many steps: take a milk bottle and pour a measured amount of bleach into it. Then take a marker and draw a line on the bottle where the bleach comes to. Fill the rest of the bottle with water before pouring it into the washing machine. Thereafter you can re-use the marked bottle. This saves dirtying an extra cup each week just to measure the bleach.

From Montreal: "I have found that bleach when added in small quantity to the last rinse water works well on white clothes for me. It soon evaporates when the clothes are dried."

INDOOR DRYING

From Kansas: "I wash—rain or shine—because I have several lines fixed up in my garage. When hanging up sheets I hang other clothes over them and they dry just as fast and this method saves clothesline space. The next day I take them in and put another load on the line. I am so used to hanging them in my garage now that I don't even think about the lines in my yard."

THE CORDUROY PROBLEM

How to wash corduroy?

I hand wash all of my small corduroy garments.

If you wash yours in a washing machine, be sure to rinse them thoroughly with either a water softener or our old housewives' friend, vinegar.

When I wash larger corduroy garments in my machine, I remove them *before* the last spin dry . . . after using the vinegar rinse. This seems to prevent hard-set wrinkles.

If you forget these steps—put them in your sink and rinse again, by hand, adding about a half-cup of vinegar to a sink full of warm water. Let soak. Plunge up and down.

Gently squeeze dry. Hang to dry. Before completely dry, take your old vegetable brush and brush the soft pile.

The vinegar rinse gives my corduroy a soft velvety shine!

And that's the way I wash my corduroy. I'm completely satisfied, but opinions differ, as my mail shows.

From Georgia: "When you wash corduroy and wring it or squeeze it by hand, it is bound to leave marks because your hand squeezes harder at different times than others. This causes wrinkles.

"It is far better to wash corduroy in the washing machine and spin it dry. The spin cycle maintains the same pressure and deep wrinkles do not form."

THE PRE-RINSE METHOD

From Washington: "I pre-rinse all loads of laundry in cold water. I just throw laundry in my washing machine, set on rinse, and let them go. After they spin, I reset my washer to fill on the regular cycle of the washing machine. This fills the machine with hot water, and I add one-fourth cup of sal soda and one-half cup of good detergent. And that's it . . .

"I really get clean clothes. No stains left.

"This removes all my stains—you name the type—especially my teenagers' dirty socks. . . . I speak from the experience of six children, from tots to teens, and we are all 'sock-walkers.' Our house is like a Dutch house —everyone's shoes are left at the door from habit, not request. We just like comfort."

SOCKS, SOCKS, SOCKS!

From Ohio: "The way to get teenagers' white socks white again is to boil them in water to which lemon slices have been added."

From New York: "This idea may help other mothers who have three or more children close together in age.

"When our children are about the same size and we wash their socks it becomes a problem as to how to separate them, whose sock belongs in whose drawer, and does this navy blue one go with that one?

"I have solved this problem by buying my youngest child all white or beige socks, the second child all red or blue or multi-colored socks, and the oldest child navy blue and dark colored.

After I do 32 pairs of socks a week, I can look at them immediately and tell to which child they belong. It certainly save me lots of time."

From Maine: "After doing five loads of laundry every Monday morning and always ending up with about five pairs of my husband's black socks which must be washed separately, I have found the easiest way to launder them.

I fill the wash basin with a small amount of liquid detergent, turn on the water faucet to make lots of bubbles and allow the hottest water possible to fill up the basin.

"Then I use a potato masher I bought to plunge up and down to wash the socks! With the potato masher I can use much hotter water, and never ruin my hands by putting them in hot water and strong detergents.

"After the wash procedure, pull the drain and let the soap suds run out. Turn on the faucet with hot water again, and let it run over the socks while the drain plug is still out.

"Close the drain again and fill with clean rinse water. Rinse in the same way, using the potato masher again.

"After this, pull the drain and let all the water flow away. Let the socks become completely cool before wringing them out. This way you have also kept the hot water off your hands again.

"Don't worry. I do *not* mash potatoes with this extra potato masher . . . just socks!

"Now can you tell us how to get the gray residue off of black socks?"

Unless your socks have been bleached—and I do not think they have, according to your letter—this gray residue is called soap film.

The cheapest, quickest, and best way I know of to remove this soap film is on that last rinse water . . . add about ¼ cup of vinegar. If your soap film is very heavy this operation may have to be repeated.

But don't waste your time doing it twice each week. For the next few weeks just rinse your socks in vinegar water. Do not rinse out this vinegar solution. After these socks are dried, the odor of vinegar will completely leave!

From Kansas City: This tip is especially useful on cool damp days when it is hard to dry heavy socks.

"I lay the socks flat on my oven rack with only *the*

pilot light on in the oven. Light-weight socks will dry in about an hour. Heavy ones will dry overnight.

"I sometimes dry underwear, in an emergency, this way in the winter. It doesn't cost anything, either, since the pilot light is on anyway, and it sure saves me lots of time."

NO MIXING, PLEASE

Never put white nylon garments in your wash with a colored garment. Even though the clothes are fast colored, the static electricity in the nylon draws the colors. White nylon should be washed with white clothes only.

SAVE WORK ON PINCH-PLEATS

When washing pinch-pleated curtains, the pinch-pleats will need very little ironing if you hang them on the clothesline right side up instead of upside down.

Fasten headings to the line with clip-type clothespins without folding them over the line. This allows the fold to form more naturally.

While still wet, "form" the pinch-pleats and fasten two or three clip type clothespins to each pleat. When dry, the pleats will hold and form beautifully. Then . . . only a touch of the iron and you'll have a job well done with less work.

TRY THIS

From Tennessee: "I fashioned a new clothespin bag after my old one with plastic screening on my sewing machine. I used a heavy duty needle and ordinary weight thread.

"I even put a couple of rows of fancy stitching along the top to dress it up!"

LET CURTAINS IRON THEMSELVES

From Iowa: "Why should women iron curtain panels? Don't they know that they can wash them and place them right back on the curtain rods while still wet? Don't gather. Just let them spread straight and take a yardstick or another curtain rod from another window and place in the bottom hem!

"The panels will dry far straighter than if they had been pressed on any ironing board.

"Starch can also be used with this method. No need to sprinkle, roll, and iron, only to have them crooked on the window. Why waste all the time and energy?"

STEP-BY-STEP WITH A DRIP-DRY DRESS

Once in a while we housewives will splurge and buy a good drip-dry dress. After we have worn it and it becomes soiled our problem is:

Shall we take the chance and wash it? Or shall we splurge again and send it to the cleaners to keep it looking nice?

In the past I have ruined many drip-dry dresses by washing them incorrectly. I feel that now I can give you an honest answer to the correct ways of washing these good dresses. I have one dress that has been washed 17 times. It was guaranteed to be drip-dry. Today it still looks perfect and has never been ironed.

Before I continue, let me remind you what drip-dry means. It means exactly what it says! It *will* drip dry! Did you know that anything will drip dry!

A dish will drip dry! An automobile will drip dry. Our hair would drip dry if we did not towel dry it, or use the dryer when we pin it up! Drip dry means exactly what it says.

Back to the dress:

The best place to wash this type of dress is the bathtub. I have found that you should fill the tub with about two inches of lukewarm water. Add some liquid detergent and mix it throughout the water. If you don't care to stoop over to wet your hands, use a plumber's plunger to mix the detergent into the water thoroughly.

Now, if your dress is stained—such as with perspiration—soak the dress in absolutely cold tap water first.

Lay the dress out full length in the bathtub in the solution. Let it remain no longer than eight minutes in the detergent water.

Take your vegetable brush or any hairbrush—and I have found a hairbrush is the best thing to use if it is clean—and holding the shoulder of the dress in your left hand, take your brush and completely "brush" the dress from the top to the bottom of the garment.

Pay special attention to the neckline marks on the collar and lapels. These areas can be given a special scrubbing. Be sure to hold your dress *underwater* when brushing these areas.

By holding the dress completely underwater as you brush, the particles of soil become loosened and the soil gets into the water. If you did not brush the dress while it was underwater, I feel that the soil would be redeposited on the other parts of the dress, causing yellowness, and discoloration.

Pull the drain plug from the bathtub. Turn on both water faucets again to get lukewarm water. Hold the dress by its neckline up under the water faucet for a moment so you will get a strong flush of water directly on the neckline. This will rinse the fibers of the material thoroughly.

Rinsing is a necessity, when it comes to getting soap film and suds from clothing. Hold the dress up after rinsing most of the suds off so that it will drain. While gathering the dress at the waistline in one hand, after the water has drained out of the tub, put the plug back in the tub and turn on the water faucet again to get more lukewarm water.

Dip the dress thoroughly into the bathtub, and again using your brush, scrub the dress from the top to the bottom thoroughly.

This may take two rinsings—according to how soiled your dress was—and if two rinsings are used, I have never found any type of material that could possibly be hurt by adding a half-cup of vinegar to the last rinse water.

This *removes* soap film. It also removes perspiration odors.

While your dress is under the last rinse water—approximately two inches deep—place a plastic coat hanger in the neck of the dress. Then and only then, while the dress is still underwater, lift it up by the neck of the coat hanger. The weight of the water will pull all wear wrinkles out of the dress itself.

While it is still dripping wet, hang it on the shower nozzle. This will allow the water to drip in the tub. Gently move the skirt if it has stuck together. Most materials do stick, so carefully place a gathered or pleated skirt into its correct position.

After 17 washings of the dress I mentioned, it has never needed to be ironed!

We have gone into lots of detail to tell you how to do this. The entire procedure only takes about three minutes. So don't think it is a difficult operation.

Remember these these when washing drip-dry articles:

Never use hot water.
Never soak too long.
Never use too much soap.
Rinse well, and hang correctly.

From Pennsylvania; "For lovely, fresh drip-dry clothes, I launder mine carefully with no unnecessary wringing either by hand or machine, and then add my liquid starch. Make starch solution light. This replaces the sizing or filler put into some materials by many manufacturers."

From Toledo: "If you hang dresses on the line by the side seam from the hem to the shoulder seam the drip dry will dry perfectly without needing ironing, especially the dark cottons. And . . . they will be wrinkle free enough to wear around the house."

I'm a working gal and take great pride in looking nice. In the spring and summer there is so much ironing to do because we wear fresh clothes every day.

I drip dry all of my dresses, blouses, and full slips on hangers. When I am ready to iron them, I sprinkle with very hot water and hang them on the shower rod on hangers. Then I drape a bedsheet around them.

In two hours they are ready to be ironed with a dry, hot iron. This requires no steam. I find they iron faster because they are dampened and they iron beautifully.

GET THE HANG OF IT

If you have found common clothespins too small for hanging heavy rugs on the clothesline, try a couple of trouser hangers.

When hanging T-shirts, put them on plastic hangers and clip the shirts at the shoulder seams to prevent blowing off the hangers.

After placing the shirt on the hanger, grab it by the shoulders—hanger and all—and shake. No ironing required, the shirt stretches longways and the neck remains the original size.

From Kansas: "When I hang out my wash, I hang my pillow cases with the open end up.

"When I bring the clothes in, I put all of the little things such as socks, wash cloths, and handkerchiefs in the pillow cases. I don't have to worry about making a trail of clothes into the house! This is especially handy in case of a sudden shower."

From Vermont: "For twelve years I have been hanging my sheets lengthwise on the line with the selvage edges together and the fold hanging down.

"The top of the sheet (which one turns back over the blanket) is clear of pin marks, and wrinkles (from holding the sheet to the line) are tucked under the mattress . . . therefore, they do not show. The rest of the sheet is very smooth and even.

"Now when my sheets wear out, they wear out all over instead of just through the middle where the clothesline gave them pressure, plus the wear in the middle from sleeping on them.

"I also take dish towels and baby blankets and pin them to the line the same way so the edges won't fray as badly."

FOR BETTER DRYING

From Chicago: "I have found when drying colored clothes in my dryer that if I turn them wrong side out they do not pick up lint from the other clothes. This also pertains to husband's socks, dark housedresses, T-shirts, etc.

"It saves me dipping a sponge into water and brushing off the lint before I iron . . . which is always a chore!"

From Los Angeles: "When removing blankets, comforters, etc. from storage, I place them in my dryer about ten minutes and let them tumble. This removes not only the odor of the moth flakes, but the wrinkles as well."

From Nevada: "I hope this hint will save housewives as much trouble and expense as it has me. This is one of my own inventions.

"I have an electric clothes dryer with a lint trap and this is the way I clean it: First, I empty the lint trap and lay it aside, then I take my husband's back-scratcher and reach in all the crevices and sides for the excess lint and it cleans it out like magic!"

From Massachusetts: "If you put only four or five items in a *pre-heated* dryer and let it run about one-half the usual time . . . then remove clothes from the dryer and place the garments on coat hangers . . . they will be almost wrinkle free!

"We are not wasting money by drying only a few garments at a time because . . . instead of running that dryer a long time we are only going to run it a few minutes!

"I find it far better to run my dryer with three, four, or five garments in it for short periods, removing them and pressing them immediately . . . than to load it up with pounds and pounds of clothes and have them all come out wrinkled!

"There is another trick to this: Use the dryer for the clock! See if you can partially touch up these garments before the next load comes out! Gals, it's fun to see if you can outwit a mechanical object. Much better than trying to outwit your husband!"

ALL ABOUT STARCH

A home economist wrote the following on starch:

"Washer starching is the fastest, most economical way to starch, if one has lots of starchable laundry.

"We have found that starch spotting most often occurs for the following reasons:

"1. A sufficient amount of starch solution is not prepared to completely cover and saturate the clean, damp items to be starched (this is particularly true in hand starching).

"2. Lumpy starch—improper preparation.

"3. The starch solution and water are not mixed well.

"4. Dampened articles (starched and dried) are not allowed to stand long *enough* to permit even distribution of moisture before ironing.

"5. Uneven starching—all too often a homemaker wishing a heavy starch finish on heavyweight fabric (such as denim or khaki) uses too heavy concentration.

"6. Some fabrics are inherently hard to finish with or without starch (particularly some rayons, linens, and dark cottons); they should be ironed when damp (right for ironing) *rather* than the usual procedure of drying, sprinkling and then ironing!

"With reference to dryer drying of starch loads: if clothes are tumbled beyond the storage dry stage, some starch will be removed from the dried clothes.

"We have found, if at all convenient to do so, the homemaker will save herself time and money if she removes the starched load from the dryer when 'right for ironing,' place in a damp towel or piece of plastic and iron at once or set aside for ironing later. By this method she saves herself the need for redampening and the time of waiting for the sprinkled clothes to be evenly damp.

"Starch that is 'sprayed on' is expensive but to the homemaker who places a premium on convenience and her time, it's hard to beat.

"1. You can spray and iron a portion of the article at a time. Most 'starchables' adapt easily to the spray method, even some you might not expect:

"Khakis—A light, even spray gives a medium stiffness. Spray and iron again if heavy stiffness is desired. (Caution: If the spray is too heavy, the starch will not penetrate as well and will 'flake off' when ironed!)

"Bedspreads, tablecloths, slipcovers, and other bulky items can be starched more economically with hot starch but they finish wonderfully well with this method too.

"2. You can spray dry articles completely, roll up, unroll, and iron at once.

"Smaller articles, and especially those made from lightweight fabrics are 'naturals' for this method. It gives the starch a moment to distribute more evenly and penetrate the fabric better.

"Blouses, skirts, play clothes, sport shirts—try this method on: strong colored dacron/cottons and other lightweight blends; solid color cottons—keep the spray fine and even; dark colors—spray and iron these from the wrong side, of course!

"3. You can spray damp-dried articles completely too, roll up, and iron immediately, or put aside for ironing later.

"Some fabrics streak readily with any starch and are always difficult to finish. Perhaps this method will help when difficulties arise.

"Dresses—solid color linens and rayons; keep the spray light to avoid excessive stiffness. If 'ironing lines' occur, brush with a damp cloth and touch up.

"4. You can hang special items on a line to spray.

"Petticoats—try hanging these on a line to spray starch. When dry, touch up with a steam iron if necessary.

"Partial starching. Want crisp collars and cuffs only? Spray the *wrong* side and *then* the right side! Then iron—first your wrong side and finish on the right side.

"No-iron net curtains—hang these on a line, too, and spray starch. When dry, touch up with a steam iron if necessary.

"Travel touch-ups? As you steam press, try very light spray of starch to remove creases and to crisp up collars and cuffs."

This is for those of you who make a big batch of cooked starch each week and want to strain it thoroughly before using so that it will not leave residue on the garments you are ironing.

Cut off an old nylon stocking about halfway up. Then pour the starch through the nylon stocking and let it drain into a bowl. This will give you perfectly strained starch.

I have found that pouring starch through tea strainers and flour sifters does *not* remove all of the sediment . . . therefore "helps" cause spots on dark clothes.

From Honolulu: "I have found the answer to streaks on clothing caused from starching.

"The method of eliminating white streaks and spots on all dark cottons is to use a gelatin solution after the usual laundering and *not* to use the starch at all!

"Use one tablespoon of plain gelatin and let it dissolve

completely in one gallon of very hot water. The hotter the water the better, for this will ensure that all the little gelatin particles are dissolved.

"The above proportions will make a light starch. For heavier materials, use one tablespoon of gelatin to only two quarts of water. I rinse my garments in the solution and roll them in a towel until excess is removed.

"This is wonderful for linens and denim and, especially, polished cottons. It leaves a beautiful polished effect again."

From Denver: "I removed 'too much' permanent-type starch from some of my white things by soaking them in rubbing alcohol until the slipperiness disappeared and then washing in hot soapy water. One must test the garment to see if it is safe to use alcohol."

From Virginia: "I wash a load of clothes almost every day and, of course, I starch some pieces. I do not throw away my leftover starch water. I pour it in a half-gallon jar and put it in the refrigerator to use the next day. I always mark the jar with adhesive tape so the children won't think it is a new kind of drink!"

From New York: "I hate to starch, so I found a way to circumvent it.

"Here's how it is done! I save up the clothes to be starched until I have a real big batch. Then I starch them with a permanent type starch and hang them outside to dry.

"This is tedious, too, but once you've done it you are set for months. I don't think is costs any more than starching every washday with ordinary starch.

"With the permanent type starch in my clothing, I find that I can put them in the dryer while they are still damp."

From Georgia: "Here's the way I starch in my washing machine: If the dial is flexible as to the amount of rinse water, you can use any amount of starch. Add the starch to cold water, mix it and then pour it into boiling water. Then pour the whole kit and caboodle into your washing machine filled with cold water.

"Don't dry your clothes and then sprinkle them as usual. Why go to all of that trouble? Just throw them in the dryer and take them out while still damp!

"Why should we waste electricity or gas drying clothes and then get them wet again? I take mine out as damp as I like them. I don't even bother to roll them—this not only sets wrinkles but uses up your energy.

"I just fling the clothes in something, anything—such as a basket, pillow case, plastic sack—and cover them with something dry, and they are ready to iron. They do iron beautifully!"

WHEN THE IRON'S HOT

From Rhode Island: "I iron when the mood strikes me. Therefore I hate to sprinkle clothes way ahead of time. I have found that I can put about four ice cubes in a washrag and place this on the end of the ironing board.

"This is excellent for spotting things that need a little bit of dampening as you iron. The terry cloth is rough enough so that it just 'swabs' the top fibers of the material. No oversprinkled spots, no going to the kitchen for another pan of water, and no wringing out the cloth each time it's dipped in a pan!"

From New York: "I have found a new way to sprinkle my weekly ironing without effort. I just dip a clean sponge in some water and squeeze it out while holding it over my pile of ironing . . . then put the sprinkled clothing back in my dryer for a little while.

"I find that this distributes the dampness perfectly without leaving some clothes too wet in spots while others are practically dry."

From Ohio: "I dampen clothes on dewy nights!

"I take down all of the unironed clothing from my clothesline and leave those to be ironed *on the line*. I let them hang until just before I go to bed.

"Then I go out and collect them and put them into my dampening bag. The dew does my sprinkling for me. A better job of dampening clothes cannot possibly be done!"

From Kansas: "When I sprinkle clothes, I use my clean whisk broom. I just dip the brush in very hot water (this will spread evenly and better) and shake the broom over the clothes. Does a beautiful sprinkling job."

From Mississippi: "Tell all of your readers that those old blankets they thought were completely worn out can be used for the most useful project in their homes.

"No matter how worn the blanket is—if it's slit, faded, or beyond repair—it's the most wonderful padding for an ironing board that you have ever used!

"The wool is not only absorbent, but downy, and it seems to absorb the steam which rises from sprinkled clothes.

"I suggest using 'your' method which said to cover the ironing board with a piece of foil—after 20 years of ironing, I have found that this is a terrific idea. The foil seems to reflect the heat and my ironing goes twice as fast. However, by putting the blanket underneath the foil, I find that I have less than half the wrinkles I used to."

From St. Louis: "Here's a tip someone gave me years ago: I have a separate pressing board. If people will cover this with a piece of chintz, there is never any lint on dark clothes!

"This kind of cover is especially good for dark cottons, navy and black, that one might wish to press on the wrong side.

"I have also found that chintz outlasts any other ironing board cover that I have ever used! One could use a pretty printed piece of chintz to match her kitchen décor.

"I find that small pieces of chintz can be found among remnants and are large enough for this purpose. Quite a saving."

From New Hampshire: "Will you ask women who iron for hours (that's me and all my neighbors) to try putting a thick bath mat under their feet when doing this tiresome chore? They won't be nearly so tired.

"I don't know what effect it has on the back but I find that the little mat absorbs something! My weight? Perhaps. But it works."

From Virginia: "When I iron my little girl's dresses, I always keep the iron about one-fourth inch from the bottom edge of a dress or skirt hem. That way, when the hem is lowered, there is not likely to be a faded white line, nor will there be a deep crease to remove."

From California: "When you put a new cotton ironing board cover on (or a clean one after you have washed it) wet it and wring it out fairly dry, then put it on the ironing board and let it dry before using.

"It will shrink slightly, fit the ironing board perfectly, and you won't have one wrinkle!"

From New Mexico: "The cord on an electric iron will not drag across the ironing board if you will slip it through a large safety pin—pinned to the cover at the square end of the ironing board."

LAUNDRYMAN'S SECRET

From California: "Here is a fast way to iron men's shirts, which I learned from a Chinese laundryman years ago:

"Iron cuffs on *inside,* going up into sleeve a little. Iron cuffs outside. Iron placket side of sleeve like flatwork. Iron other side of sleeve. Repeat the same process on the second sleeve.

"Iron *inside* front facings, stretching the one with the button-holes in it a little (if necessary to get it flat). Iron the *inside* of pockets lightly.

"Iron *underneath* side of collar; iron top side of collar.

"Fold back yoke over toward front (if no yoke, then about 'so far' down the back). Now iron, going over the shoulder to the front—it works like flatwork!

"Lay the body of the shirt flat on the ironing board, inside facing up, with seam away from you at the far edge of the board. Iron the back on the inside. Lay the front over and iron like flatwork!

"Repeat with the side nearest you.

"Fold collar and press lightly again on *outside*.

"Put shirt on hanger or fold.

"This takes three to four minutes to iron one shirt, once you learn the routine. Naturally, short-sleeved sports shirts are a little easier than dress shirts. The trick is treating it as much like flatwork as possible!"

KEEP IRON IN CONDITION

From Ohio: "To clean the bottom of an iron: Put a piece of brown paper on your ironing board (a large paper bag will do nicely) and sprinkle it generously with table salt.

"Slide your heated iron around and around in the salt and all of the dirt, stains and other marks will completely disappear.

"The iron should then be 'slid' over a double thickness of wax paper. The wax paper method also removes any stickiness you may have on your iron.

"To clean the top of the iron, just rub with a silver polish when the iron is cold and you will have a shiny iron again."

From New Jersey: "I use baking soda slightly dampened on a cloth or sponge to remove the starch from the bottom of my *cold* iron. There is no need to scratch the bottom of the iron with other methods."

From Kentucky: "Whenever it rains, I catch rain water and use it in my steam iron. I place a piece of cotton in a funnel and pour the water through it to catch any sediment that it might contain. The soft rain water works better than water from the tap."

From West Virginia: "For those who have electric ironers . . . we found the reason that ours was not ironing well was that it had six different pieces of cloth on it and each one sagged and wrinkled (and this made lumps).

"Take off all the old covering down to the padded base covering that fits tight on the roller.

"Buy the *cheapest* muslin you can find so that it *will* shrink, cut and hem as wide as the roller, then pin one side of the cloth across the roller.

"Pull the cloth tight around it and clamp the ironer down. Pin this as tight as you can. Then cut off the extra material so that it does not overlap too much.

"Sew this by hand as tight as you can and fasten the edges in a few places. Now take a wet press cloth and run it *through* your ironer *several* times and you will have a tight fitting cover, just like the new ones. By running the wet cloth through the ironer it shrinks the muslin a bit and it is skin-tight, thus avoiding puckers and wrinkles."

8.

Bake-Day Bliss

~~~~~~

LET 'EM EAT CAKE!

From New Jersey: "For 40 years I lined my cake pans with double thicknesses of brown paper. Recently I have used aluminum foil for lining and find it better. The paper-lined cakes usually had a burnt crust but I have yet to find one burned that was lined with foil.

"As most of my children are married I find that regular cake pans are too large so I save one-pound coffee cans and bake my cakes in these. After baking and cooking, I wash and reline the tins with fresh foil and put the lids on and they keep beautifully until ready to use for baking again."

Ladies! After receiving this letter I took six one-pound coffee cans and a box of ready prepared cake mix (*adding* one-fourth cup of salad oil) and baked the cutest cakes you've ever seen.

And here's another idea I came across after being too tired to ice them.

I removed the cakes after baking and stacked the layers one on top of the other—with a piece of foil between each—and placed in a big coffee can. Then I put them in my deep freeze.

This not only saves foil but keeps the frost off my homemade cake, takes up less room in my deep freeze, and I can spot exactly what it is because I labeled on the top "chocolate cake" with a felt marker.

When icing these cakes *if* you are one who has a very sweet tooth you can take a knife and cut each layer crosswise again, thus removing one, two, or even three layers of cake and ice between each layer.

Here's something else I found out: never remove just two layers of this cake when icing one cake. Why not ice two at the same time and put back in the deep freeze? Then the next time you want cake all you have to do is remove the cake, let it thaw and eat. Most icing recipes call for enough batter to ice an entire cake. Therefore half recipes—so I find—are hard to make.

If you want your cakes to look nice and high (like the pictures in the advertisements) use eight-inch cake pans rather than nine-inch pans. Makes all the difference in the world.

Sifting cake mixes before adding the liquid saves overtime beating to get the lumps out.

From Tennessee: "Instead of just adding eggs to my cakes, I separate them, drop in the yellows and beat the whites separately. These whites should then be folded gently into the cake batter. This makes lighter and higher cakes."

From West Virginia: "Here is a quick way to get rid of air bubbles in a cake.

"When the batter is in the pan and ready for the oven, drop each pan on a table from about six inches high. You will see all the bubbles break on the surface of the cake batter.

"Do this three or four times to each cake pan and when you are finished the product will be smooth and hole-free."

From New York: "When I make an angel food cake from a boxed mix, I pour it into the pan and put a few drops of food coloring on top of the dough. Then I use a knife and 'cut' the coloring into the batter. It makes a beautiful marble cake."

An angel food cake will slice easily without crumbling after being frozen at least 24 hours and then thawed.

When removing a cake from the oven, place the cake pan on a damp cloth for a few minutes. This makes the cake come loose from the pan and helps prevent sticking.

Always cool a cake fresh from the oven, while still in the pan, on a cake rack or grill of some sort. Allows the heat to escape.

From Chicago: "I never bake a boxed cake in layer pans anymore.

"I now use tomato cans, vegetable cans, even coffee cans. The small-size cakes, individual tiny cakes, etc., can be cooled and put into the deep freeze for use any time of the day or night!

"You are exactly right when you said never make just

one cake at a time. I found that I can always make enough for two cakes at a time, pour in the batter and load down my deep freeze with these darlings.

"When the time comes that I am tired (but still want cake) all I have to do is . . . remove that old tin can full of delicacies from my deep freeze, let it thaw and ice it.

"The icing requires little effort. It is the original making of the batter that dirties my kitchen.

"Another thing . . . if you do not have time to make icing—ice cream, synthetic whipped cream or fruits may be placed on top of the cake and it's called a fancy dessert these days!"

Does everybody know the old trick of adding a pinch of baking powder to powdered sugar icings? This prevents hardening and cracking and the icing will stay moist and "gooey."

When icing a cake (either cooked or powdered sugar icing), if you will dip the knife in hot water before spreading the icing, it will go on smooth and will not stick to the knife.

From North Dakota: "I love to decorate cakes and not being professional, I found that a piece of string or thread, dipped in a little cake coloring and laid gently across a cake is great. Be sure the string is a little longer than the width of your cake. Pick up the string each time and continue making tick-tack-toe marks across the icing. Makes a mighty pretty cake."

From New Jersey: "Using a child's paint brush and food coloring, you can decorate cake icing. With the basic food colors, you can mix any color and your design can be as elaborate or simple as you wish.

"A butter frosting makes a good base and I would suggest lightly sketching your design with a toothpick on the icing before tinting it."

When making cupcakes for lunch boxes or for picnics, instead of icing the tops, split the cupcakes across the middle and put the frosting on the inside. When the tops are put back, the cupcakes are then ready to travel safely.

CUT DOWN STIRRING TIME

From California: "When making boxed puddings that require cooking . . . rather than stand over a hot stove for umpteen minutes, stirring and stirring, mix the dry pudding with one egg and set it aside.

"Put the milk in a heavy, heavy pan on the stove. When the milk almost reaches the boiling point, turn down the heat and pour the pudding mixture into the milk, stirring briskly.

"Result? Smooth pudding in about 30 seconds.

"I use a rubber scraper for the entire operation and I feel it works better than a spoon and affords a good way to scrape out the bowl in which the pudding mix has been cooked. None is wasted.

"I vary vanilla pudding by adding sliced bananas, drained canned pineapple or any type of cut up chocolate candy bar after the pudding has cooled a bit. If color is wanted in any pudding, I add halved maraschino cherries . . . either in the pudding or on top of it.

"Often I add small marshmallows to chocolate pudding after it cooks a bit."

From Delaware: "I wonder how many people know the quick way to cook prepared puddings?

"Measure the two cups of cold milk into the saucepan as usual. Take out one-half cup of the milk and put into a bowl.

"Mix the pudding mixture into the half-cup of cold milk and put the saucepan with the remaining milk over low heat. When the milk is fairly hot, stir the pudding mixture into the hot milk and in a few seconds it is thickened!

"I admit there is an extra bowl to wash but to me it is a timesaver as I detest standing over a stove, waiting and stirring."

FOIL THOSE COOKIE SHEETS

Instead of lining cookie sheets with foil, try using foil alone. To do this, remove the rack from your oven before turning on the heat.

Tear a piece of foil the size you need . . . being careful to leave about a two-inch space on all sides. Now place this sheet of foil on the oven rack. Place whatever you are going to bake on the foil and return rack, food and foil to the hot oven.

When food is done, take your pot holders and remove rack and all and place on top of the range to cool. This works for cookies, biscuits, turnovers, frozen French-fried foods, and any recipe that calls for a cookie sheet. Saves buying and storing cookie sheets, too.

From Ohio: "After years of messy hands from greasing cookie sheets and cake pans with a scrap of waxed paper or paper towel, I've discovered that a waxed paper sandwich bag ends all my troubles.

"Just slip your hand into the waxed paper bag, with the seam side up! This forms a little 'greasing glove' and will keep you from being left with shortening under your nails and on your hands."

From Oregon: "When rolling out cookie dough, I use powdered sugar in place of flour on my board and I also dip the cookie cutter in the same sugar. (Be sure the powdered sugar is sifted before using it.)

"The cookies will look and taste better, and the dough which must be refolded does not get as heavy as it does when rolled with flour."

From Georgia: "I have learned how to get mass production all by myself when baking cookies.

"I cover my cookie sheet with several layers of foil and

when one batch of cookies is cooked, I remove the top sheet of foil and set it aside to cool and refill the cookie sheet with another round of cookies.

"Also . . . the grill from your barbecue can be used as a cooling rack."

"I keep my homemade cookies nice and fresh by putting a slice of fresh bread in the cookie jar with them. I change the bread about every other day."

"When my can of shortening is almost empty and I cannot even measure out a half of a cup, I use it only for greasing cookie sheets and cake pans, or when using mixes and refrigerated cookies. Then if a few crumbs from the previous batch of cookies get into the shortening it doesn't matter at all."

From Nevada: "I used to use butter and oleo wrappers to grease cake pans and cookie sheets and often wondered why my cookies and cakes stuck to the pans or came out in pieces.

"One day, I had to use a vegetable shortening to grease pans and my cakes came out of the pan perfectly. The oleo wrappers are fine to grease candy pans."

TO MAKE A BETTER "BUTTER" . . .

Back in the old days—when I was young—many of us could not afford pure butter and so we had to use oleo. In those days, it came in a white brick and we put the yellow coloring in it. We had to mix it ourselves. Today it is already colored. But one mixing trick of those days is still good.

I used to put two pounds of oleo in my mixing bowl and let it sit until the oleo was fairly soft. Then I placed this in the electric mixer, let it whip for about five minutes, turned the beater on low speed, and added one small can of condensed milk. I creamed this slowly so as not to spatter the liquid, then turned the mixer on high speed and whipped until it was nice and creamy. I later found out that if I had no canned milk, plain milk would do. I always added a dash of salt to make it taste more like grandmother's home country butter.

The whipped oleo was then poured back into the original box. (Nowadays we have to put a rubber band around some oleo boxes, in order to hold them together, as they are not sealed.) Then the oleo was put in the refrigerator and let sit a day or so to harden. This made the creamiest oleo you ever put in your mouth.

When I wanted to be real fancy, or was having a party, I would pour the soft creamed oleo into little molds, set it in my refrigerator for a while, and presto . . . I had the cutest little pat of butter you've ever seen!

For family use, this whipped creamed "butter" (oleo) can be put into ordinary coffee cups to set. The cup can be turned over, placed on a little dish and the butter knife laid along the side. If you're feeling artistic, you could make large molds out of the creamed oleo and carve little designs on the top with the end of an ordinary teaspoon.

So next time you don't have anything to do (and I am wondering when that will be), set aside a pound or two of oleo and try this method.

From Connecticut: "For those 'party' butter pats . . . I took a raw potato and cut a darling design in it with my fluted edge potato cutter (any design or initials can be carved into the flat side of a potato) and pressed the designs onto softened butter slices. The butter pats were adorable.

"Place slices on waxed paper first, then press design on. Place paper in refrigerator or deep freeze until needed. And while you are making them, make lots. They keep for a long time if frozen."

Use a vegetable peeler to shave off thin curls from a firm or frozen stick of butter. Almost instantly the curls will be soft enough to spread.

MUFFIN SECRET—MIXING

From New York: "The secret for making muffins is in the mixing.

"The batter must be stirred, never beaten. The dry ingredients are only thoroughly moistened and at this stage the mixture will appear lumpy and rough. When the muffins are overbeaten, everything goes wrong and an inferior product results.

"Grease the pan on the bottom only as an aid to better volume."

KEEP YOUR DONUTS IN SHAPE

To make donuts that don't lose their shape when you fry them, try this: After you've cut them out, place each donut on a square of aluminum foil slightly larger than the donut itself with a hole punched in the bottom of the foil so the hot fat can drain.

When ready to fry the donuts, drop donut, foil and all, in the fat. When fried, pick out the foil with a pair of tongs.

You will have perfect donuts every time and you can use this foil over and over again.

WHEN YOUR FAMILY'S PIE-EYED

Here is a trick for making fruit and berry pies:

Fix all your fruit for one or more pies as usual, adding sugar and your favorite seasoning.

Line a pie tin with waxed paper. Fill the pan with the pie filling and freeze. Later . . . *remove* the frozen berries from the pie pan and store in the freezer, after wrapping, and use this pie pan again and again.

Now . . . when you want a pie, make your crust as usual and line the pan with the dough, remove paper from the frozen pie filling, and just slip the frozen pie filling in. Cover the top with crust and bake!

No thawing out and adding sugar, etc., later.

If the filling for your berry pie seems a little too sweet or flat . . . add the juice of one-half lemon! This not only takes away the too-sweet taste but brings out the flavor of the berries.

Food coloring can always be added to cherries when baking pies. I add a few drops of red coloring into my thickening. It makes it look just like the professionals!

From New York: "For those who freeze homemade unbaked pie shells in their home freezer: I have much better luck if I allow the uncooked shell to thaw completely before baking."

"When I am baking a pie I always place my pan with my pie in it in a larger pan when getting ready to bake it. Thus if the contents runs over, the goop will go into the larger pan rather than onto my oven."

From Colorado: "I always roll my pie crust between pieces of waxed paper, measured—so that by rolling to the edges of the paper I have the *exact* size I want."

From Louisiana: "When I make pastry for pie crust— even the ready mix type—I add a pinch or two of baking powder to the dry ingredients before adding the water and mixing it.

"Somehow or other, it seems to make the pastry so flaky—as if it were rolled in layers, and it is so good!"

Another secret on making a crisp pie crust, from California:

"When a recipe calls for so many spoons of water, take the time to use ice water instead of using tap water. If you do not keep ice water in your refrigerator, put a few cubes of ice in a glass of water until the water is chilled and use this.

"And instead of using your hands to mix the pie dough as our mothers did, cut the fat into the flour with two knives (better yet, use a cold meat fork, as it mixes four times as fast).

"I have found that by using the hands, the heat from them causes the pie dough to be tough.

"Another handy little idea which a neighbor suggested: never pour the spoons of water in one spot on the flour and shortening mixture. Shake the spoons of water loosely above all the flour mixture. Dough mixes easier."

From Kansas: "When baking a pie shell I tear up a narrow strip of aluminum foil and cover the edges of the pie crust. When the shell bakes the edge will not burn at all, but it will still get brown.

"The foil should be removed immediately when taking the shell from the oven, to avoid sogginess."

From New Mexico: "For crushing vanilla wafers (I much prefer these for crusts, no sugar needed and not crumbly after baked) or graham crackers . . . I put them into a waxed bag and tape it closed. I squeeze all of the air out of the bag before taping. Then I crush the wafers with a rolling pin or my hand."

From Arizona: "The secret in making meringues is to let the egg whites warm up before beating them and to always spread them on a hot filling. This will prevent leakage!

"Also . . . if you add one teaspoon of water for each egg white, it will increase the volume and make the meringue more tender. I use only two tablespoons of sugar for each egg white after the whites have been beaten to the 'frothy' stage."

From Montreal: "When I cut a meringue-topped pie I simply grease my knife and the meringue never tears! The oil on the knife will allow for a perfect cut every time."

VARIETY IS SPICE OF BROWN-AND-SERVE ROLLS

Brown-and-serve rolls can be prepared in many ways. Sprinkle them with a little water to give them a different texture. Or split them open before baking and insert butter or oleo that has been mixed with paprika! The shortening can be mixed with onion powder, too, to produce onion rolls. Garlic can be used, and again add the paprika. Raisins can be soaked in hot water so they will be soft. Split the rolls and insert some of these raisins.

Now for that "something different." Make a thick paste

of powdered sugar and water and add some rum extract. You can add a little oleo but it is not necessary. Spread this paste on top of hot rolls. Delicious! This is called a hot rum roll. When you can afford pecans, stuff some broken nuts between the folds. Always add butter or oleo in the folds of the rolls. If you can't afford pecans, use peanuts or you may put some peanut butter in the folds with the oleo or butter.

Best of all are apricots! Cook dried apricots (be sure to add lots of sugar and lemon juice) and when they become a jam, spread between the folds. Be sure to put lots of butter or oleo on top of the buns.

Cinnamon, when added with sugar, is wonderful. Mix this with some butter or oleo and make a paste. Spread between folds and put a dab on top. Luscious!

When baking biscuits, put the biscuits around the outside of the baking sheet. Leave the inside part of the sheet *bare* in order that the heat may radiate and all of the biscuits will be evenly browned.

Take a carton of canned biscuits and cut them in fourths with a pair of scissors.

Drop the little pieces of the canned biscuit in hot fat to which has been added cinnamon and fry. Drain on paper. Top with sugar if your taste calls for it. Quick and easy for breakfast. These cinnamon biscuits are terrif.

If you like your sweet rolls warmed for breakfast and use a skillet to warm them, here's a trick:

Place a lettuce leaf in the skillet and put your sweet roll on top of the leaf and then heat. The roll will get piping hot without charring on the bottom, and the lettuce will leave absolutely no taste.

To reheat biscuits or rolls to the right temperature for the dinner table, put them in the top of a double boiler, cover with aluminum foil, and then place the lid on top. This will prevent the moisture which usually accumulates on the inside of the lid from dripping on the biscuits and making them soggy.

From New York: "Would you like to know how I always have homemade biscuits at a moment's notice?

"Every week I make up about four times my regular recipe of biscuit dough and bake them until they rise . . . and are just beginning to turn brown. When cool, I package them and store them in plastic bags in my freezer.

"If company comes, or my family has a yen for biscuits before my eyes are open in the morning . . . I just run the biscuits into my hot oven to finish browning!"

Try this! Heat a ceramic tile in the oven when you bake or warm dinner rolls. Then place it on top of the napkin in your bread basket before putting in the rolls.

Not only does it keep the grease from soiling the napkin but it also keeps the rolls warm until the last one is eaten!

BREAD CRUMB SUBSTITUTE

From Pennsylvania: "My mother occasionally runs out of bread crumbs. Here's what she did the last time this happened:

"She had a bag of prepared stuffing—the kind which is already mixed and seasoned—and she put this in her blender until it was finely ground up and used this for bread crumbs.

"The chops tasted so good when breaded with this mixture that now we always have pork chops, veal chops, and so forth breaded with finely ground herb stuffing."

Now isn't this just the greatest?

If you would like such a mixture to bread chops in, you could also save stale bread and throw in a little sage or poultry seasoning!

And while we're on this subject, if you ever need dry bread and do not have any, it is best made by laying it on the racks in your oven *without* foil. When the oven is turned on, the bread dries out thoroughly from *both* sides and is ever so crisp.

From Canada: "I used to give loaves of dry bread to an elderly lady who I thought would use it for dressing, but she told me to wrap it in a damp towel and leave it in the refrigerator for a couple of days, then remove the towel and heat the bread in the oven. It is as fresh and crispy as the day it was baked. It takes only a few minutes to heat. This also can be done with rolls."

From Nevada: "Unsliced loaves of very soft French bread sometimes dry out before you get half way through them . . . and a whole loaf that is frozen is hard to slice.

"If I know I cannot use this bread quickly, I slice it while it is nice and fresh, and freeze it in its own bag or a plastic bag, removing individual slices as needed. Thawing a slice or two takes but a short time.

"Why not keep six or seven slices from fresh loaves of different kinds of bread frozen in plastic bags and 'ready to go'? You can keep several different kinds going in the bread box this way."

SECRET OF GOOD PANCAKES—EGGS

Often, complaints come in that boxed pancakes are not as light, high, and fluffy as grandmother's old-fashioned recipe. The answer I found to this after much experimenting was:

When a recipe calls for one egg this means the average egg. Some of us buy small size eggs because they are cheaper. In this case, I found that if I used two eggs instead of one . . . the pancakes were much higher and fluffier!

The second reason I found was that anytime a pancake batter called for eggs, the same recipe was much better if the yolk was put into the batter and the white beaten separately until stiff, then gently folded into the batter. There was all the difference in the world when using the same recipe if the eggs were divided this way!

When the original recipe called for two eggs, I used three eggs, whether the recipe was boxed or home-made. The pancakes were absolutely lush! They were light, stood much higher, and when you cut them with a fork they did not become "gooey." Yes, eggs are expensive, I know. But we must get them into our stomach some way, so why not put them into that batter?

I found it both time and energy saving, and had fewer dirty pans, beaters, etc., when I *doubled the pancake recipe.*

I used three iron skillets at the same time, placing one on each burner of the stove. You can tell when the pans are ready for the batter by putting your finger under the water faucet, getting a few drops of water on it, and holding it above the skillet. If the drops of water bounce around when falling to the skillets, start cooking.

After the family was fed and while the skillets were still hot I cooked the rest of the pancakes but didn't get them quite as brown.

Next, I got some paper napkins out. As each pancake was cooked, I placed it between the sheets of the paper napkin. The paper napkin allowed for some of the steam to escape from the pancake.

I stacked these in batches of threes, then folded a different colored napkin around the outside of the three pancakes and placed them in plastic bags. They were now ready for the deep freezer. Those of you who do not have deep freezers may put them where the ice tray ordinarily rests.

So make up an extra batch of pancakes and the next time your family wants pancakes remove as many as you will need and pop them in your toaster! Not only is this time saving, but I found the hotcakes even *better,* as they were crisper than when they were originally cooked. This is also a dandy snack to have in the refrigerator when our little tykes get hungry.

Do not make your pancakes any larger than a piece of bread. But they must be at least this large because if you make them too small they will not pop up out of the toaster!

Those who do not like sweets such as syrup on their pancakes . . . have you ever tried cranberry sauce? It sure is different. Apple sauce—straight from the can—is excellent too, especially the red sauce.

SWEET TALK

When you buy sugar put it in an old coffee pot. You can pour this any time you need it without spilling!

From California: "To soften hardened sugar, I preheat the oven to 350 degrees, turn the heat off and place the bag of sugar (not the box), as it is, in the oven, close the door, and as soon as the bag begins to get warm the sugar will soften and will not be damaged in any way!"

From New York: "Once in a while, we have a box of brown sugar, or a bag of granulated sugar that is as hard as a rock. I have tried using a hammer to break this, but with no results. Heretofore, I have always ended up by throwing out the sugar. Recently, I discovered that it can be utilized to its fullest.

"I now put the 'brick' of sugar in a pan and pour boiling water over it. This will melt the sugar. Let it sit a few hours, turning the block of sugar over from time to time as it dissolves. This gives you nothing but liquid sugar, but this can be boiled on your stove to make the most delicious homemade syrup for waffles and pancakes that you have ever tasted.

"I vary this by putting it in separate bottles and adding different imitation flavors to the various bottles. In one bottle I add a few drops of maple flavoring; in another bottle, I add a few drops of plain vanilla; in the next bottle I add imitation cherry flavoring! This flavoring is usually put in cakes and cake icing, and one day I just happened to pick up the bottle and put some in the syrup. It is out of this world!

"Any of these flavors may be added to either brown or white sugar. I just boil the sugar and water until it gets sort of thick. You can tell this because you will have slow bubbles breaking on top of the mixture while it is cooking. After utilizing a bag of what I thought was lost sugar, I now buy sugar and make all of my own syrup."

CONSIDER YOUR CONDIMENTS

From Delaware: "Have you ever noticed how paprika, chili powder, dry mustard, and curry powder tend to turn a dark color once they have been opened for use and then replaced on the shelf?

"Well, try keeping them in the refrigerator! These condiments will hold their true color indefinitely if placed back in the refrigerator after each use."

From New Hampshire: "To save money, I buy large jars of mustard and salad dressing. Then when planning a picnic, I fill baby food jars from the large jars. If the baby food containers have the screw type caps, they are just perfect!"

From Nevada: "When you go on a picnic or barbecue things at home, use the cups of your muffin tin to hold pickles, sliced onions, relish, salt, peanuts, mustard, sliced tomatoes etc.

"By using the muffin tin you can carry eight different items to the table at one time. Only one pan to wash, too!

"Also, for that same barbecue, I cook my hamburger patties beforehand and wrap them individually in foil. When it comes time to eat them, put the whole package in the hot coals and they will be steaming in a jiffy. They are never burned and dry."

From Ohio: "I pour a little vinegar into all my empty mayonnaise and mustard jars and shake vigorously until the jars are clean. Then I put the mixture aside until I make potato salad or cole slaw. This is one way to utilize what is left in these jars.

"I add only water to get all the good out of the catsup bottle. I always add the 'catsup-water' to my vegetable soups, spaghetti sauce, chili con carne or anything else made with tomatoes, as we usually have to add water anyway."

From Florida: "For something different, try adding orange juice or a little vanilla extract to peanut butter until it is slightly thin. Cream well. The taste is delightful!"

BAG THOSE WALNUTS

From Michigan: "I just discovered a neat trick for cracking walnuts that will keep the shells from flying all over the room, and I must share it with you.

"Spread a paper on a table. Then use a board on which to crack the nuts.

"Place the nut just inside the opening of an old plastic bag such as vegetables or buns come in. Crack each nut while it is *inside* the bag, then push it to the bottom of the bag.

"When you have cracked eight or ten nuts . . . pour them out on the paper and just pick out the meats. Push shells to one side and proceed as before. There will be no shells to sweep up and no mess in your kitchen!"

Phenomenal! I used a hammer to crack pecans this way. I also found that a regular nutcracker will do the same thing.

But the most amazing thing about the procedure is that you can shake the bag the cracked nuts are in . . . before emptying it on the paper . . . and most of the shells will separate from the meat. And sure enough, for the first time I cracked nuts and had no shells all over the chair and floor.

QUICK SUBSTITUTE

Did you ever run out of cocoa and have no chocolate for your children's milk? Use chocolate pudding! Add two teaspoons in a glass and then add your milk. It's delicious.

This is wonderful hot, too. Just heat your milk and pour a dab of it into the bottom of the cup first, stir into a thick paste, and finish filling up the cup with the hot milk.

COFFEE BREAK

For instant coffee drinkers who do not drink too much coffee and find it caked in the jar . . . just pour hot water into the jar and dissolve the caked coffee and place it in refrigerator. When you need it, just pour a small amount into the cup and add boiling water.

From Hollywood: "I keep the sediment from coffee (and have a coffee pot that is very easy to clean) by lining the basket of my percolator with a tissue. Cut to fit your coffee basket.

"Just push the middle of a tissue over the middle post into the coffee basket itself. Put the coffee in.

"It is very easy to dispose of the grounds this way, and the percolator stays clean."

When emptying a can of coffee into a canister, pour from the back side *toward* you and very little coffee will spill.

Never throw away any leftover coffee. When it's cool put it in an ice tray and make coffee ice cubes out of it.

When you have your afternoon snack, use these cubes instead of plain ice when making your iced coffee. Keeps the real taste of coffee and prevents weakness caused by melting ice.

These cubes may be put in plastic bags if you are short of ice trays. Just hit the bag on side of sink and they will crack loose.

TEA TIME

From Texas: "Iced tea is wonderful on hot days. Here's the way I vary it: when I make two cups of freshly brewed tea I add two spoons of raspberry or strawberry jam! I stir this well and then pour it over the ice cubes."

I would like to let you in on a secret of an easy way to make iced tea from tea bags.

In the morning while I am doing my breakfast dishes, I always take two or three tea bags and put them in the bottom of a fruit jar.

When the water from the faucet gets hot I fill the jar about halfway up and cover the tea bags. Take a spoon and push the bags down into the water so that they will not float. Put the cap on the jar and set aside.

You will find that your tea will not cloud, will not be bitter, and you will utilize all the tea.

Another little hint which a friend of mine gave me: this jar can be filled up again and more tea made from the same tea bags! I did not know this, but it works. Even the second jar of tea is not bitter. No mess, no dirty pans, and no bother. Worth giving it a whirl if you drink iced tea!

Ever tried putting a caramel candy in a cup of hot tea? It's excellent! Not only does it give a little different taste to the tea, but it takes the place of the sugar and cream which you ordinarily add.

9.

Rise and Shine!

━━━━━━━━━━━━━━━━━━━━━━━━━━━━━━━━━━━━━━

FOR SPARKLING WINDOWS—KEROSENE!

I have washed windows with about every product on the market and have made a wonderful new discovery: kerosene!

I have weighed time and energy against results and here is the answer to that equation.

I tested and found that the insides of windows are loaded with carbon. This comes from cooking in the kitchen, heating systems, cigarette smoke, etc. This gummy substance is hard to remove and is what causes streaks! I did not find carbon on the outside of the windows. I found dust. The dust which floats in the air adheres to the outside of the windows and when it rains we get water spots.

Now here's my wonderful new discovery:

Take a small container (a small plastic waste basket is wonderful) and pour a quart of very warm water into it. Add one-half cup of kerosene. (This may be bought at your filling station. You can buy as little as a pint.) The kerosene will float on top of the water!

Take an old but clean wash rag and dip it in this water mixture. Gently squeeze it out. Not *too* much, though. You do not want it dry. You only want to keep the water from drip, drip, dripping . . .

Gently wipe (no energy required) your windows in a circular motion. Watch the soil loosen!

After the window is washed, take a clean bath towel and just wipe over it. Don't try to use an old piece of sheet. I found that the terry cloth bath towel absorbs the carbon and dirt which the kerosene has loosened immediately. There is no need to rub it hard. Just use the towel as if you were dusting a piece of furniture. Don't waste your energy when it's not necessary.

The first time you wipe your bath towel across your kerosene-washed window, you will hear a little squeak. You might see a few little residuals from the bath towel that look like lint. Forget it. The second time you wipe over the window, every bit of it will be gone!

You will have no lint on your window regardless of how sloppy you are when using this method. Neither have I ever found a streak . . . inside or out. If you didn't do anything but get rid of those streaks, that's worth something, eh?

Another thing I have found about this method is that when raindrops or water splatters from the garden hose hit the window they actually "bead" and roll right off like on the hood of a car after you have just had a 20-dollar wax job!

I also found that the little coat of film that the kerosene left not only protected but kept dust particles from sticking. It's the most amazing thing you have ever seen. A pint of kerosene costs less than a dime and will wash approximately 18 windows. What more can you ask for a dime?

Now, here's another little hint for tired, too busy mothers who have big houses:

Stop and think. When you walk in your house . . .

which part of the window do you see? The bottom part, of course! So why clean the top part every time you clean the bottom? Better to conserve your energy and wash the bottoms more often and have them clean. The venetian blind or shade usually covers the top part anyway.

I also suggest that you wash the inside of the window twice as often as the outside, too. It's twice as dirty. It accumulates more carbon and soil.

And while you are at it—as you remove screens to wash the windows, wash them, too. There is really no point in washing windows if you are going to put back dirty screens.

If you are pressed for time and energy and must have windows clean . . . don't overlook the possibility of *dusting* the inside of windows with a clean cloth. (This naturally is not for greasy windows.)

"Dry dusting" of windows will leave no streaks, will remove a surprising amount of soil and cut down considerably on the frequency of washing.

THOSE "NUISANCE" JOBS

A broiler grill can be a nuisance to clean, but needn't be if you follow this plan:

Do not wait until the grill is cold and the burn has set. Following the preparation of food, immediately empty the grease and sprinkle the top of the grill with powdered soap and cover with wet paper towels and add a little water. If you are not one who buys paper towels, use a piece of newspaper.

The steam that occurs and the soap do most of the work for you while you eat!

From Nevada: "When I use my roaster, I always line the bottom of it with foil, and place another piece over the meat rack. Then I punch holes in the foil where the holes in the rack are! The roaster is much easier to clean and works just as well."

From New Jersey: "The one thing that is really hard to wash is charred shishkebab skewers. I have found that if I push them through a soap-filled pad before the pad is wet, they come clean quick as a flash, with no trouble. Wash as usual."

From Georgia: "Buy an inexpensive jelly roll tin in the dime store. Line this with foil, and sprinkle it freely with salt. Use this as a drip tray under overflowing pie filling or scalloped potatoes.

"Result: no smoking, no burning, no messy oven! Just fold up the foil and throw out, replacing with a clean sheet."

From Massachusetts: "While I am frying things I turn those throw-away pie tins upside down over the other burners on my stove and it keeps them clean. The tins are much easier to clean than the burners."

From Michigan: "To prevent burns and heat spots on my drainboard . . . I just keep a cake rack sitting on the counter at all times. The little space between the rack and the drainboard has prevented all blisters and damage. Racks cost so little in comparison to a new drainboard."

From Kentucky: "I make handy hot pads to protect my drainboard top. I use pieces of corrugated pasteboard cut the size and shape I desire. I make two thicknesses of these and then cover them with heavy-duty foil and replace the covers as they get worn or torn."

From New York: "I clean my kitchen walls and ceilings with my sponge floor mop. I find that this works beautifully if I use frequent changes of suds and rinse water. A bonus: the stretching exercise is good for the figure."

From Washington: "For those who have sticky wooden salad bowls: I have found that when my bowls were covered by this residue, the only thing left to do was purchase a fine grade of sandpaper . . . and start sanding. Sand with the grain, if possible, and continue until all the residue is gone.

"I then use a clear waterproof spar varnish and apply it lightly. There is no taste from the varnish. My salad bowls always look like new."

From Maine: "If milk or any other food sticks in your pots and pans while cooking . . . just sprinkle enough cleansing powder (such as we use in our kitchen sinks) and cover it with water. Leave the pot overnight.

"By the next day, the stuck food will be all loosened without any effort."

From Virginia: "For those of us who still use the old-fashioned dish rags . . . the very last thing I do at night in my kitchen is clean the sink with a cleanser which contains bleach. My dish rag has bleach on it and I do not rinse it, just leave it in a corner of the sink overnight. The next morning I rinse it and have a very bright clean rag."

Nylon net scrubs potatoes far better than a potato brush. Nylon net also can be used to make a wonderful soap-saving bag for those little pieces of soap. This little soap bag scrubs cleaner as well as being easier to hold onto when taking a shower than an ordinary slippery cake of soap!

Use wax paper instead of that dust pan. Tear off a piece and place it between your feet, sweep the dirt onto it and then wad it up before throwing it in the wastebasket so that the wastebasket won't get dirty.

From Milwaukee: "Here is a little trick I use to keep most of the dirt from collecting under my refrigerator and other appliances in my kitchen which are about two inches from the floor:

"I bought an extra piece of linoleum and cut it to fit underneath each appliance. I slide this underneath the heavy items which a housewife cannot ordinarily move. When it's time to clean, I reach underneath the appliance and pull the linoleum out, wash it off, and slide it under again."

From Chicago: "I bought a small sponge and stapled it to the end of my yardstick. (You could use tacks if you did not have a stapler.)

"This reaches under and in back of my refrigerator and all of the low furniture and so forth. Cleans without moving the heavy appliance."

From Idaho: "For a long time I have tried to buy smooth-surfaced table mats because food particles adhere to the raised pattern on the linen finished ones.

"Finally I covered the ones I own with contact paper. This gives me the color and surface I want and they are much easier to clean."

When narrow-necked crystal vases and bottles need cleaning and a bottle brush won't do the work, break several egg shells into the bottle or vase, and add a little water, and shake until all film and dust disappears from the glass. After rinsing, the vase will be crystal clear.

RE-USE THOSE PLASTIC BOTTLES

Never throw those little plastic squeeze bottles away. They have so many uses.

For over a year now I have filled them with pine oil disinfectants. I put one on the kitchen sink, one on each bathtub, and leave one on the shelf above the washing machine.

The tops of the little bottles can be twisted out with a knife. When the top is removed you will see a long plastic tube the length of the bottle. Just pull this tube out and discard it. Fill bottle with pine oil and put top back.

In the kitchen I use mine everytime I pick up my sponge (to wipe the drainboard). Just dampen sponge, squeeze a small amount of disinfectant on it and wipe. Bugs aren't even supposed to walk where a disinfectant has been used. This idea eliminates odors and picks up grease at the same time.

I also clean my stove with this after frying, to pick up the spattered grease.

When you come across a dirty collar or a dirty spot on those clothes just spray a dab on and either scrub with a clean vegetable brush or rub between hands.

The plastic bottle of disinfectant in my bathroom is used for washing the tub and sink. Toilet bowls can also be cleaned with this.

By using these little bottles, instead of the big ones, we have eliminated many steps and problems. No more messy bottles to break or rusty cans of cleanser. The little plastic bottle looks neat. It's also there right where you need it and not under the sink in another room. This saves energy and time.

Don't throw away your next liquid detergent bottle before you rinse it out. Do you know that you can put a little warm water in that bottle, swish it around a bit and you will get another sink full of free suds?

If you always measure your soap and detergents before using them, you will be amazed how much longer a box will last.

Know those old plastic bleach jugs? There are many uses for them.

I have found that I can cut off the top of one of these jugs and use the jug for a garbage collector in my sink. I heat the end of my icepick over the gas burner on the stove and after the end of my icepick gets hot (and don't do this with a new icepick unless you are *sure* it's guaranteed because some icepicks are no good after you heat them), you can take this red hot poker and stick it through the bottom of that wonderful bleach jug and it will allow the water and drainage to go right on down that old sink.

After all we don't throw our garbage away every minute do we? It takes us (I figure) about two hours to fix our supper, eat it, and wash the dishes. So keep one of these beautiful plastic jugs (cut off about six inches high) in your kitchen sink. After all the watery substance has drained off your vegetables, etc., dump it in your garbage, turn on the water faucet, and rinse that plastic container out. Leave it in your sink. You are going to use it tomorrow, tomorrow, and tomorrow once you get used to it.

I have also found—by accident—that these big plastic jars are excellent to keep lettuce in, if you punch a few holes in the bottom of the jug. Know why? They fit a head of lettuce! Exactly. Also . . . with a few holes punched in the bottom . . . any excess moisture will leak out and prevent that goop from forming! (I am sure that all you gals know what that goop is.) The plastic container is very sanitary, you can cut it any size you want to, and it will keep your lettuce from bruising, while cooling in your refrigerator.

But best of all it's free. When you can utilize something, don't ever throw it away.

THE HANDY HANDLE

Recently I discovered one of the greatest things in this whole world of housekeeping. It's how to use a pot with a handle for mixing things!

I have only three mixing bowls. All were in use at the time. It came time to mix cornpone . . . makes not one bit of difference if I have been mixing cake batter, biscuit mix or mashed potatoes . . . it still works.

Don't use mixing bowls. Use your big pot with the handle. The one in which you usually boil potatoes. It's got a handle! This is worth its weight in gold.

I never thought about having to grip with all of my fingers to hold that old mixing bowl before; the pan with the handle sure saves lots of energy (this is good for those who have arthritis or are just plain lazy!). Ladies, the pot with that handle doesn't turn around and doesn't take one bit more water or soap to wash (besides, you have the handle to hold onto while washing it).

And, think this over . . . usually you are making up those biscuits or that pie dough before you need the old favorite pan anyway. Rinse it under the faucet and use it again for the next item.

I even used it with my electric mixer. The handle "held" the pot still while I turned on my beater. It's deep and the potatoes didn't spatter. I just hate to clean spattered creamed potatoes off my wall and it will happen nearly every time they are put in your regular bowl . . . or at least it does for me.

Try mixing things in a pot with a handle. You have nothing to lose. Pick a deep pan. It's the best. And do you know what? The top part of that old double boiler (which we seldom use) is wonderful for this type of mixing, too.

HOW TO CLEAN ALUMINUM TUMBLERS

From Colorado: "Would you please tell me how to clean my silver-type aluminum tumblers?

"I have rubbed them with soap pads until my fingernails are absolutely gone, tried all kinds of aluminum cleaners and the *inside* of the tumblers are the biggest mess you've ever seen.

"These are not new but are a good quality and we love them, especially for cold drinks. The inside of them is all dark and the outside doesn't look any better."

I borrowed six darkened aluminum goblets from one of my neighbors.

I, too, tried soap pads and scouring powders. But I found I also lost not only manicures but about three fingernails!

Here is my very simple answer to the problem:

Fill a very large pot—preferably aluminum—with hot water. (Later I will tell you why I suggest you use aluminum.) I dumped two heaping tablespoons of cream of tartar into the water after it started boiling. Then I put in the aluminum goblets. They were hammered on the outside and had a rough texture.

I let these boil until the aluminum turned clean and all of the dark spots were gone. I kept the water at a rolling boil all of the time. This took about 30 minutes but I imagine the length of time would depend on how much "build-up" you had on your own aluminum goblets.

If you cannot get all of your goblets in the pot at once, put in as many as you can and then take your tongs and remove them as each becomes clean, set them in your sink, and add the others. I used the mixture over and over again.

After this operation I found it shined the goblets if I took a thoroughly dampened soap pad and went over them gently, rinsed with hot water and dried.

Before I dumped the water out, I took all of my neighbor's little aluminum pans and put them in this big container and let them boil also. Result? Shiny pans, and all the discoloration was gone. I also buffed this gently with a soap-filled pad.

Now, here is really the reason I asked you to use a big aluminum pot:

It got the pot clean at the same time. Don't waste energy by doing one thing at a time when you can kill two birds with the same stone!

To clean aluminum when it turns black . . . I boil grapefruit skins and lemon skins in the pot with a little water. I boil this for at least one half-hour or until the black is gone.

Empty the pot and all that is needed is a slight scouring with a soap-filled pad. No more broken fingernails for me!

SHOO, FLY!

From Georgia: "Here's a tip that is a contribution from my husband.

"To keep flies away from the garbage can, all one needs to do is to slightly coat the bottom of the can (which has first been cleaned) with oil which is drained from your car, after you make an oil change. My husband changes the oil in the car himself, but I am sure that your favorite gas station attendant would save some of the drained oil for you. We stumbled onto this little tip by accident and, surprisingly, flies hate the oil! This coat of oil also helps to prevent rust on the bottom of your garbage can."

From Boston: "When we see a line of wretched ants coming through our kitchen door, we take a bit of white chalk and draw a line on the floor or kitchen bench or wherever the ants are marching through—and the good old saying is, 'An ant will *never* cross a *chalk line!*'

"This works just beautifully. We draw a chalk line also around the sugar canister and cake tin and the ants do not pass the line, and the chalk can be easily rubbed off later."

DOUBLE DUTY

From Texas: "Here's how I make my own garbage bags:

"Take three double sheets of a newspaper and close on the fold, then fold again. Use your sewing machine and stitch along the folded newspaper starting at the right folded edge. Sew down one side, across the bottom and up the other side.

"You will have a strong bag about 11 x 14 inches. Put your hand inside of the bag and close it in 'fist' fashion. Presto, the bag opens and you have the most beautiful garbage bag in the world!

"This is just the thing for your garbage pail and you will never need to line that old garbage pail again . . . and don't you hate that job? You will never use a store bag again. I can even pour in that half-cup of coffee with the grounds. The 'newsbag' never comes apart and never leaks.

"I find this is an excellent way to get rid of my old newspapers at the same time. I sew stacks of them at one time."

From Oklahoma: "My stove has a small space between it and another appliance. I have had much trouble with this because of food dripping down into the tiny space and spilling.

"I took a yardstick and cut it the correct length, covered it with several layers of aluminum foil, folding it over and over lengthwise. I slip the yardstick between the two appliances and when it becomes greasy all I do is remove it and replace the foil."

GIVE IT A TRY . . .

From Delaware: "I whiten my wooden breadboard by rubbing it with a sliced lemon which has been dipped into a dash of salt! After rubbing it well with the cut side of the lemon, I rinse it in clear water under the faucet. I then set this in my kitchen window to dry. And do you know, it bleaches itself white!"

To make a quick economical cutting board . . . use several thicknesses of newspaper and cover with a paper towel. No mess to clean up.

Add a nutcracker to your list of the most useful things in your kitchen. A nutcracker is wonderful for opening stuck bottle caps, etc., even fingernail polish bottles.

A handy tool is a "whitewash" or calsomine brush to be used as a dust brush or regular whisk brush. This cheap paint brush is soft but thick, and gets up spills or any trash for a quick clean-up. It also gets in corners and does not leave broken straws to pick up.

SHARP AND SHINY

From Idaho: "I keep my kitchen shears bright as new by rubbing them with a few drops of cooking oil after each use.

"If they are already rusted, dip a soap-filled pad in oil and rub. Most of the rust will come off."

Did you also know that steel wool dipped in kerosene will remove rust spots from tools and the like?

I wonder how often we women use a knife in the kitchen when a pair of clean kitchen shears or an old pair of scissors would work better? I especially like shears to cut up cold, leftover meat for casseroles, and to cut slices of bread into squares for crumbs. I have also used them to cut up snap beans and to dice celery. Next time, try shears. You can always go back to the knife.

From New Jersey: "The best way I know to sharpen kitchen knives is to buy a plain metal file at any hardware store. These metal files are wonderful as they leave just enough rough edge on the blade of any kitchen knife to actually cut through the skin of a tomato, apple, etc., which a smooth blade won't do as well.

"When my husband sharpens my knives he gets all the little fancy, smooth gadgets out and sharpens them as if he were honing a razor blade. I have found this is not the type of edge that belongs on kitchen knives.

"I suggest that women buy the smallest file they can find. They are inexpensive. By buying a very small one (perhaps four inches long) it can be kept in the kitchen drawer along with the knives themselves. That's where it really belongs."

IDEAS, IDEAS, IDEAS

From Nevada: "The most indispensable tool in my kitchen is my slotted egg (or pancake) turner—the end of which is on a slight diagonal—for stirring gravies. Nothing can beat it because of the enormous surface (compared to a spoon) that scrapes the bottom of the pan or skillet. It takes a lot less strokes to do a much better job."

From Toronto: "If you will put a few drops of salad oil—whatever kind you use—on your rotary egg beater once in a while, it will make it turn smoother . . . and you will find that the salad oil will not taste in your food."

From California: "I find nylon net very handy as a fine strainer . . . since my metal ones tend to rust and the plastic ones aren't fine enough.

"Also, since my husband prefers loose tea, I take a large square of the net and fold it to make several layers of thickness. I then fold it like an envelope and fill it with tea and close it with a pin or a couple of basting stitches. This makes a large tea bag for a large pitcher of tea. The tea bag can be used two or three times and it can be refilled."

Keep an eye dropper handy near your kitchen cabinet to use to measure vanilla. Otherwise, when poured from the bottle itself, a "drop" often becomes a "blop" and the food is ruined.

From Kentucky: "I would like to pass on my method of utilizing burned food—and that does happen in every household.

"Set the burned kettle or pot containing the food immediately in a larger container holding cold water. Do not stir the food. Leave uncovered.

"When the food has cooled, pour the contents of the pan into another one. Do *not* scrape with a spoon. I find that any of the scorched food will adhere to the pan in which it was burned, thus eliminating the burnt taste."

Necessity *is* the mother of invention!

Being not only a mother . . . but without soap pads, scouring pads, soda, cream of tartar, and everything else to clean a burned pan while on a recent vacation, I ran across something different.

Know what it was? It was that old suede brush! Yep, the very one we use to clean our suede shoes.

I burned a pan, *but good*. I filled it up with hot water and a little liquid detergent and let it sit overnight. The next morning, the roast and the potatoes were still stuck! My fingernails and my kitchen knife would not remove it.

Then daylight dawned upon me. There was nothing in the house but my suede brush. As a last resort, I used it, and if that's not the best scouring brush I ever used! This brush has a wooden back on it so it did not even ruin the polish on my fingernails!

Gals, I suppose you all have an old suede brush in the house. And even if it is your best one, who cares? These brushes can be washed easily and laid in the kitchen window to dry. They can be bought in your dime and department stores and are very inexpensive.

GIVE KITCHEN CABINETS A LIFT!

From Denver: "When kitchen cabinets have become hopelessly yellow, buy vinyl adhesive-backed paper and cover them.

"My husband and I covered ours in 'birch.' It cost

about five dollars and everyone thinks we have new kitchen cabinets.

"Remove the handles first, overlap the edges cutting a 'V' for the corners and it is the easiest thing in the world to do. If bubbles occur, prick them with a needle and press the air out.

"As a matter of fact, three years ago we did our kitchen walls above the tile. It cost us one-quarter of what a paper hanger had quoted for the job.

"Our bathroom cost us even less. Three years later they are still perfect and I even use scouring powder on the soiled spots. We are delighted. We even did the drawer fronts on the drawers under our sink."

If kitchen cabinet doors won't stay shut, place a small piece of adhesive tape on the top edge of the door to make a "bind." The tape will not show on the top edge of the door. This may be the place a grip is needed. If the door is very loose, two layers of tape may be necessary.

A shoe bag hung on the inside of a lower kitchen cabinet door is just the thing!

It gets all those awful extra gadgets out of that upper kitchen drawer that make it so cluttered, you can't find your favorite knife.

This will hold those big spoons (that you seldom use but must have), gravy ladles, spatulas, screwdrivers, pliers, bottle openers, and just about everything.

MORE BRIGHT IDEAS

From Michigan: "Those little one-inch magnets are the 'brains' of our house. They can be bought at any dime store.

"We use 'em to anchor reminder notes on the refrigerator door, the stove, the instrument panel of the car, or any old place that's metal and that we think might be a likely place to 'jolt' us at the right time.

"Saves lots of arguments and is very convenient in many ways."

From Louisiana: "I have found that people can make their own blackboard . . . any size or shape . . . by buying a piece of plywood or wallboard. Purchase a can of 'blackboard paint' and paint the plywood or wallboard with three coats of this. Let dry between coats. To wash this clean, use a damp sponge."

If you will coat the covers of cook books with clean shellac, drips and spills will wash off easily!

For those who have "mass" silver polishing to do and use liquid silver polish, try this: Cut out four-inch squares of worn sheeting or such—ten or twelve at a time—and put them in a shallow glass baking dish.

"Pour the liquid silver polish over these cloths. Leave long enough to wet the cloth. Turn the little pieces of material so that the silver polish soaks through the fibers.

"After soaking these, store them either in a jar or wrap them in a plastic bag. Whenever a fork needs touching up—after eggs, ugh!—take one of these little cloths and polish it.

"These little squares last for three or four touch-up jobs. Even if the cloths dry out, they still work. This sure, safe method can be done when you are doing your dishes, and your silver will always look nice."

If you keep an opened block of camphor in your silverware chest and on the shelves of your glass door china hutch . . . you will not need to polish silverware so often.

Rubber should not come in contact with silver. Never put a rubber band around any silver or you will get a permanent stain.

When packing paper plates for a picnic, put a sheet of wax paper between each plate. Then serve the meal right on the wax paper. Lift it off afterwards . . . and you have a clean plate for dessert!

When a pot or pan of grease catches fire, the first impulse usually is to grab the thing and run to the sink and throw water on it. This is bad as it only spreads the grease and might spatter.

If grease in a skillet catches fire, first turn off the heat; then, if possible, put a cover on the skillet, maybe using a long-handled fork.

Baking soda sprinkled over the fire smothers it. Never use flour.

If the fire is in the oven turn off the heat and close the door. This usually shuts off the air and smothers it.

From Texas: "When I buy a box of soap-filled pads I take my scissors and cut them in fourths. I do an entire box at one time.

"A fourth of a pad is just enough to clean one or two pots or pans. I find this much better than using the whole pad at a time as it is too much waste."

From Montana: "I wrap my soap-filled scouring pads in foil after using them. I find that this keeps them from rusting."

From New York: "To help save on soap-filled pads, soak them in liquid detergent after rinsing. Keeps them from getting rusty and they always have soap in them."

From Oregon: "I have asphalt tile floors and my kitchen chairs scratched them so badly that I had new tile laid recently. Then I took an old felt hat of my husband's and cut little circles to fit the base of each leg, and glued them on.

"Now, when we scoot chairs back and forth, they leave no mark on my new tile."

From Missouri: "I use pillow slips for chair backs in my kitchen, over my plastic and chrome set. Sure is cool in summer. Easy to remove and wash, too."

Do you know that if you glue a rubber fruit jar ring on the bottom of your dog's eating bowl, it won't slip and slide across the waxed floor in your kitchen?

From Connecticut: "To copy a recipe from a newspaper, cover it with a piece of ordinary wax paper, and rub the wax paper with the edge of an ordinary table knife, back and forth. The print will transfer itself to the wax paper.

"Remove the wax paper and place it on a recipe card or any white paper and again rub with the knife itself. The print will then rub off and adhere to the white card. The newspaper print will look as if it had been stamped on the recipe card!

"Steady the wax paper with your thumb and forefinger. I use the blade portion of my knife right below its tip. I find that it is best to hold the knife at about a 45-degree angle. Gentle pressure is sufficient. You will find that if you use the very tip of the knife or press too hard your paper will tear.

"When using the above method the article can be transferred only once.

"I move the knife back and forth very swiftly when doing this—it takes only a few seconds. The cutest part of it all is children can have fun by making transfers from the comic pages. The color also transfers itself to the white paper. Sure keeps kiddies busy on bad days."

From Cleveland: "Quite by accident one day, I happened to lay a glass pie dish on my recipe book and immediately happened to notice how it magnified the printing of the recipe. Yes, I wear glasses! But it magnified it more.

"Now, instead of covering my recipe book with a piece of plastic to keep it clean—which most housewives never have the time to do anyway—I just lay my glass pie plate over the recipe book itself and not only does it keep the book clean but I can even read the printing without my glasses! Some glass dishes may not magnify, but mine does."

From New York: "I take plastic bags that protect cleaned garments, wash them, and when dry, cut them in squares. I then use them to wrap things for the refrigerator and deep freeze. One can use them over and over."

KEEP PICNIC FARE COOL

From Connecticut: "For those who do not have ice chests and must go picknicking with ordinary old baskets, let me say that wonderful refrigeration can be obtained by putting crushed ice cubes in a plastic bag —naturally, without holes—twisting the top of the bag eight or ten times, then tying a knot in it!

"These ice bags can be put in the bottom of the basket which has been lined with a piece of foil. Place your food on top of these ice bags. You will find when it is time for your picnic that your food will be crispy, fresh, and cool.

"The water in these bags can be used to wash the kids' hands and faces. Also to clean up your silver."

IF YOU WEAR RUBBER GLOVES

From Hollywood: "The best way I have found to preserve rubber gloves is to hang them up separately by the edge of the cuff. I use clip-type clothespins on a wire hanger in my kitchen. My gloves last much longer."

From Honolulu: "I have been annoyed countless times by having to discard one rubber glove because I have worn a hole in the other glove. It always seems to be the same hand that wears out first. Matching did seem impossible until one day, quite by accident, I remedied the problem by turning the glove with the hole in it inside out.

"When I tried to put it on later I thought I had two gloves for the same hand. I then discovered what had happened and realized that in the future I could just turn the leftover glove inside out and match it with another leftover one and have a new pair!"

From Montreal: "I have brittle fingernails and must wear rubber gloves when doing dishes, laundry, etc. I pull off little pieces of cotton and saturate them with my favorite fingernail oil and drop one in each fingertip and leave it there. Now I don't have to oil my nails every night."

MAKE THE MOST OF SPACE

From Kansas: "I have limited space on my drainboard, so my husband nailed a breadbox to the bottom of one of our cupboards above the drainboard.

"It is so much easier to reach up and open the bread-box now than it was to lean across the drainboard. It is also nice to have it up out of the way and have the extra space below.

"A word of caution: If the ventilation holes in the box are covered by the wall, the bread will mold rapidly. This can be corrected by punching more holes in the breadbox where the air can get in it."

HOME-MADE CANISTERS

From New Hampshire: "We never had a suitable canister set until we made our own out of two pound coffee cans. We painted these to match our kitchen, then labeled each one with the name of what each one contained.

"We placed a seal in the middle of the lid for decoration and sprayed the whole can with a spray plastic for sealing and waterproofing. This is very inexpensive and can be done to suit your own color choice."

STOCKING UP

From New Jersey: "Did you know that nylon stockings are great to put those packages of foodstuffs into before storing them in the deep freeze?

"I find that tubing made from nylon stockings will

keep packages from sticking to one another. The foot and top of the stocking may be cut off, leaving a beautiful nylon tubing. Just slip your wrapped, frozen packages and boxes into this tube."

DON'T BE FLOORED BY THE JOB!

From Missouri: "I want to tell you how intrigued I am by the way my friend sweeps her kitchen floor. She does no bending down over a dust pan!

"She had a carpenter saw a space in the floor directly inside her closet door. Into this space which is nine inches by three inches, the carpenter fitted a box to match the incision.

"Now all she has to do is open her closet door and sweep the kitchen litter into the little box. You see, no bending at all! When the box needs emptying, she removes the box and empties the sweepings into a waste basket."

I may be called Maharani of the floormop . . . but there can be pleasure in mopping floors! I love it myself.

Mops should never be dirty. "Cleanliness is next to godliness." Keep your mops clean. Not only will they not smell, but it will be a pleasure to pick up that beautiful white thing with a handle and mop your floors . . . if it is clean.

I have learned that there are many ways to bleach a mop. The best is to put a little suds and bleach in a

bucket—better yet, use that plastic waste basket, and bleach *it* at the same time—and let the mop soak. Don't use too much bleach. Rinse and dry in the sun.

For those of you who have washing machines like mine (semi-automatic and the hose runs to your wash tub) don't waste that good sudsy bleach water. Set your plastic bucket under your hose where the water drains out. Place your mop in this bucket. As the washing machine empties those beautiful hot suds . . . let it run over the mop.

Now, don't remove. Just leave the mop there. And here's why: As you rinse your clothes . . . the mop will rinse itself! You have a thoroughly clean mop and no effort on your part was taken to wash it.

To save wax and time, use an old wet mop to wax all floors. It goes on smooth and even.

Wash mop in warm soapy water when through. Rinse and let dry. All of the wax will come out.

Liquid wax is easily applied on floors and linoleum if you will use an inexpensive paint brush for the job. This is easy to apply and there is no waste whatsoever.

From Louisiana: "When I wax floors, I also wax the feet of the chairs and rockers, and then they do not mar the freshly waxed floors."

From Florida: "If you find it necessary to get down on your knees, whether it be for scrubbing, painting floors, waxing or what-not . . . sew pockets on an old pair of slacks just where the knees are. Then insert a large sponge in each square pocket and presto . . . you have built-in kneeling pads!"

CLEANING PLASTIC CONTAINERS

I have had so many complaints on the stains and odors in polyethylene (plastic) containers that I have had an interview with an authority on the subject. Here's what she had to say:

"I have used and sold these containers for years. Most of the complaints sent in on these containers are due to the lack of information received by the customer.

"Our company recommends that thorough washing with detergents regularly will usually keep polyethelyene canisters clean. However, if orange juice, tomato juice, or iced tea leaves a stain, merely wash, rinse and fill with a mild bleach and water solution, let stand overnight, and the next morning the container will be nice and white again. Bleach will not harm it.

"Onions, which we like to have on hand, all chopped up ready for hamburgers, remaining in your sealed container in the refrigerator for several days may leave the 'fragrance' lingering.

"Just wash your polyethelyene container in hot suds, rinse and dry, then crumple a piece of black and white newsprint into the container, seal and leave overnight. The next morning—no odor!

"The black printer's ink on the newspaper will absorb the odors from the polyethelyene. The porousness of the newspaper helps, too. Don't use colored sections, or a page from a magazine."

From Honolulu: "After trying different methods of removing stains from my plastic dinnerware, without results, I decided to try paste-type silver polish. It works just beautifully.

"It takes a little elbow grease, but you can do the silverware at the same time! Wash and rinse as usual.

"I also found that old toothbrushes are the greatest little scrubbers for those hard-to-get-at places—faucets in the kitchen and bathroom sinks, etc."

LEMON AIDE

Don't throw away lemon halves after the juice has been extracted.

They may be dipped in salt and rubbed on the bottom of your copper-bottomed pots for a few minutes and they will gleam like new. Then pick up a soap-filled pad and scour the bottom of the pot lightly. This will leave a film of "jeweler's rouge" on the pot, which will help prevent further accumulation.

EASY DOES IT

Let me tell you a good way to remove bubble gum from fabrics: Chew another piece of bubble gum until all the sweetness is gone out of it. Then use this piece of gum to pick off the gum in the garment. The garment should be chilled beforehand.

Was anyone unkind enough to leave a burning cigarette on one of your china saucers? To remove the nicotine spot, just dip a cork into some moist salt and the spot will come right off after rubbing.

From Kansas: "I use cream of tartar on a dampened washcloth to clean my porcelain surfaces.

"Sometimes when I am out of the cream of tartar I

use hydrogen peroxide. This removes rust from the surfaces and I find that it whitens the porcelain."

From Washington: "I use a glass coffee server to boil water for instant coffee and deposits collect on it quite rapidly. Here is the method I use to keep it sparkling:

"Boil vinegar in the pot once a week and the lime deposits will dissolve like magic. Save the vinegar. It can be used over and over again. Wash and rinse the pot well."

From Kentucky: "Our new chrome fixtures were becoming dull with water deposit build-ups and not wanting to use cleansers, I tried this:

"I soaked a terry cloth in vinegar and 'snuggled' it all around, over and under the faucets, then literally poured more vinegar over the cloth and let it soak for an hour.

"Besides removing the spots from our faucets and so forth it also loosens all leftover cleanser in the hard to get at places. Afterwards . . . just rinse and the chrome is bright as new again!"

From West Virginia: "For those who do not like tarnished forks caused by potato salad, eggs, etc., I have found that whether I clean the table or not, if I pick up the forks or any silver items that have touched eggs, and immediately place them under water, tarnish does not occur.

"Usually all I do as soon as breakfast is over is pick up the four forks, fill up a glass with water, and place the forks in the water. Anything else we happen to have, such as mashed potatoes, that might stick to the tines of the fork is loosened by the time I get ready to do the dishes."

From Arizona: "In regard to stains on stainless steel:

"At our church we keep a small cloth saturated with

real butter in an ice box dish in the refrigerator. After cleaning the sinks with this cloth, we then take a dry cloth and polish them. This removes all of our stains and our sinks are pretty."

"Have you ever tried using toothpaste on copper and stainless steel? It sure cleans it.

(Numbers refer to paragraph)

Ball point ink, 1

Blood, 2

Collar lines, 3

Fingernail polish, 4

Lipstick, 5

Makeup marks, 6

Milk and Cream, 7

Mucous, 8

Mustard, 9

Napkin stains, 10

Paraffin, 11

Rug spills, 12

Rust, 13

Scorch, 14

Shine, 15

Sweater knots, 16

Under-arm odors, 17

Yellow treated cottons, 18

10.

Heloise's Handy Stain-Remover Guide

▪▪

In the kitchen is where most stains are removed or are apt to happen. Be prepared. Never let a spot remain any length of time. (Time sets most stains and the quicker you can give 'em first aid . . . the easier they are to delete.)

There is a Handy Stain-Remover Guide in my earlier book, *Heloise's Housekeeping Hints*. Like a few additional quickies?

One can always send to the The Superintendent of Documents, Government Printing Office, Washington 25, D.C. and for 15 cents ask for a booklet called "Removing Stains From Fabrics." It's complete.

While you are waiting: Here are a few hints . . .

Always work from the *back* of a piece of fabric when using *liquids* to remove a stain. Why liquefy the stain and spread it through clean non-damaged fibers? Place material on absorbent towel, etc., then pour fluid through. Stain will dissolve on under towel. Replace with a clean portion and continue until stain is removed, etc.

When working on stains with absorbent *powders* always work from the *front* of the fabric where the damage is. Powders "absorb" damage . . . so get to it where the damage occurred . . . and quickly!

*Note: * means . . . spot test on hidden part of fabric*

first to see if it is safe for material and follow directions on product.

1. *Ball point ink:* Some impossible! Try rubbing alcohol* first. Or, fingernail cuticle remover.* Or, amyl acetate* (drug store). Apply with wash cloth and rub.

2. *Blood:* Flush with cold water.* Soak in ¼ cup of salt* and 2 cups cold water. Wash* and rinse as usual.

Meat tenderizer* when mixed with cold water and applied as a paste will often dissolve blood. Allow to set until blood dissolves then wash as usual.

Peroxide* (3%) is often useful if applicable.

3. *Collar lines:* Men's and women's shirts. Take dimestore chalk,* draw heavy line across soiled area, let set overnight. Wash* as usual.

4. *Fingernail polish:* Amyl acetate* (drug store) should be sponged on with piece of cotton. Pour amyl acetate on cotton and rub from back of material. When underneath absorbing rag is soiled and discolored, replace with clean portion.

5. *Lipstick:* Use pure glycerine,* pure detergent,* cleaning fluids* or rubbing alcohol if safe for fabric. Work in fabric, let set, then wash.*

6. *Makeup Marks:* Usually powder and rouge on dark necklines of garments. Dip washcloth in white vinegar,* wring out *well* and wipe soiled spot.

7. *Milk and Cream:* Wash in neutral detergent* suds and warm water.* Rinse.* Cleaning fluid* can also be used.

8. *Mucous:* Soak in ¼ cup of salt* to each quart of warm water.* Cleaning fluids* may sometimes be necessary if vomit contains butter fats. Wash as usual.*

9. *Mustard:* Work glycerine* into stain and let set, then detergent.* Bleaches* and alcohol* are sometimes necessary to remove remaining stains.

10. *Napkin stains:* Wet white linen or cotton napkin, apply scouring powders which say "contains bleach"*

and rub with brush. Let set and rinse.* Cleaning fluid* is sometimes necessary to remove grease.

11. *Paraffin:* (wax) Scrape off as much as possible after it solidifies. Iron between white paper napkins with warm iron or tissues until all excess disappears. Cleaning fluids are also useful after above procedure.

12. *Rug spills:* Blot up as much moisture as possible. Cover with clean towel, step on damp spot, twist foot until all moisture is gone. Cover with clean dry white towel and weight down with books for at least 24 hours. This prevents spotting but does not remove ink, etc. First aid only.

13. *Rust:* Use commercial rust removers.* Or one tablespoon of oxalic acid* (drug store) in one cup of hot water* if applicable to fabric. Rinse in baking soda* water.

14. *Scorch:* A cloth dipped in 3% peroxide* and used as a pressing cloth removes most scorches. Household bleaches* can also be used.

15. *Shine:* Dip wash rag in white vinegar.* Wring out thoroughly. Rub material briskly, and hard. Let dry. Do not iron. Some professional cleaners use sandpaper! But . . . it removes some of the fibers.

16. *Sweater knots:* Use fine sandpaper and just sand away! Will remove knots and sweater will look like new.

17. *Under-arm odors:* Caused from bacteria. Wash* garment in neutral detergent* and rinse in one cup white vinegar* to one gallon of water. Let soak* if possible, an hour or so.

18. *Yellow treated cottons:* Never use regular household bleaches. Remove dingy stains with commercial color removers* bought at dime and drug stores. Soak garment in 140° water* with remover* only until water discolors. Remove garment and make new solution for second application if necessary. Use commercial nylon brighteners* when washing thereafter.

Index

Aluminum, *see* Cleaning

Ammonia, 45-46

Angel Food Cake, *see* Cake

Ants, keeping away, 152

Apple Sauce: Fluff, 25-26; on pancakes, 134

Aprons, 65

Bacon: crumbled, 30; floured, 30

Baking Powder: in cake icing, 120; in pie crust, 128

Baking Soda: cleaning iron with, 115; cleaning oven door with, 48; cleaning plastic ware with, 44-45; cleaning waffle iron with, 54; in scalding chicken, 61; to smother fire, 159

Bananas: refrigerating of, 91; slicing of, 91; whipped, 26

Beans: dry, 87-88; pole, 85

Beef: chuck roast steak, 12-13; left-over steak, 17; rib eye, 10; roast beef steak, 10; swiss steak, 27; tenderizing of, 10, 16-17; with spaghetti sauce, 17

Blender, chopping chores of, 53

Bread: freezing of, 132-133; French, 132; refreshening of, 132

Breadboard, whitening of, 153

Breadbox, 162-163

Bread Crumbs, 132

Broiler Grill, *see* Cleaning

Brown Sugar, *see* Sugar

Bubble Gum, removing from clothing, 167

Burned Food, making edible, 155-156

Burn-Free Broiling, 17

Butter: as stain remover, 168-169; pats, 125-126; shaving to spread, 126; whipped oleo as, 124-125

Cabbage Slaw, 76-77

Cabinets, Kitchen, 156-157, *see also* Cleaning

Cake: 117-120; Angel Food, 119

Camphor, 159

Canned Goods, shelving for, 1-3

Cannisters, 163

Carbon, 46

Celery Tops, 77-79

Chair Coverings: Bath mat, 67; shag rug, 66

Chalk, *see* Ants

Cheese: and macaroni, 31; grating of, 31; refrigerating of, 31; slivering of, 31

Chicken: and dumplings, 61; basting with mayonnaise, 61-62; boiled, 58-60; frozen cooked, 18; on toast, 60; scalding, 61, *see also* Sandwich Fillings

Chili: freezing in quantity, 16; making from meat loaf, 16

Chives, *see* Onion

Chocolate Milk, 137-138

175

Cleaning: aluminum, 150-151; behind appliances, 146; broiler grill, 143; burned pots, 159; ceilings, 144; chrome, 168; coffee pot, 168; copper pots, 167; dish rags, 145; egg beater, 155; electric skillet, 53; iron, 115; kitchen cupboards, 4-9; kitchen shears 154; oven, 45-48; plastic containers, 166-167; plastic ware, 44-45, 167; porcelain, 167-168; salad bowl, 145; silver, 158; stainless steel, 168-169; screens, 143; shishkebab skewers, 144; vases, 146; waffle iron, 54; walls, 141-143; windows, 146

Clothespin Bag, 100

Coffee, 138-139, see also Gravy

Condiments: for picnics, 136; seasoning roast with, 11; storing of, 3, 136

Contact Paper: lining shelves with, 6; on bathroom walls, 157; on kitchen cabinets, 156-157; on table mats, 146

Cook Books, 158

Cookies: Cake Icing, 26; keeping fresh, 124; mass producing, 123-124

Corduroy, see Washing

Corn Bread, see Turkey

Corn Meal, frying pork chops in, 27

Corn Starch, 36

Cranberry: salad, 92; sauce on pancakes, 134

Cream of Tartar: cleaning aluminum with, 150-151; cleaning porcelain with, 167

Cucumbers, 81

Cupcakes, 121

Curtains, 101

Cutting Board,, 153

Dampening, 111-112

Defrosting, see Refrigerator

Detergent: "built vs non-built,"

95; bleach content of, 95; premeasuring, 96, 148

Dish Cloths: cleaning of, 145; making of, 69

Dish Towels, see Towels

Dog Bowl, 160

Donuts, 126-127

Double Boiler, 86

Drainboard, 144

Drip-Dry: curtains, 101; ironing, 104; hanging, 103-104; starching, 104, see also Washing

Drying, 96, 99-100, 105-106, see also Electric Dryer

Eggs: baked, 35, 37; boiled, 34-35; frozen, 32-33; fried, 35-37; in pancakes, 133; pickled, 38-39; poached, 35-36, 37; separating, 35; with chicken on toast, 60

Egg Shells, 146

Electric Dishwasher, 40-44

Electric Dryer, 105-107; removing blanket storage odors, 106, see also Lint

Electric Ironer, 115-116

Electric Skillet, see Cleaning

Eye Dropper, as vanilla measure, 155

Felt, 160

File, as knife sharpener, 154-155

Filter, see Lint

Fire: putting out grease, 159; putting out oven, 159

Flies, see Oil, Motor

Foil: baking pie on, 128-129; cookie sheet, 122-123; cooking sausage on, 29; cooking turkey with, 56; crack filling with, 153; drip tray, 144; freezing cake in, 117; freezing sausage in, 20; frying donuts on, 126-127; hot pad, 144; lining cake pans with, 117; lining freezer shelves with, 52; lining ironing board with, 112-113; lining roaster with, 143-144; poaching eggs on, 36; shelf lining, 5-6; 8-9; mass producing hamburger, 14; storing left-overs in, 51-52; wrapping hamburger patties in, 136; wrapping ice cream in, 27; wrapping soap pads in, 159; under milk cartons, 52

Food Coloring: in berry pie, 127; in eggs, 35

Fruit Cocktail, 92, *see also* Gelatin

Garbage Bags, 152-153
Garbage Disposal Unit, 45
Garlic, *see* Pork
Gelatin: and fruit, 21, 22; as starch, 109-110; dessert, 22; kept in jar, 20-21; salad, 21-22
Grapefruit, 92, *see also* Cleaning, aluminum
Grease, easy-to-pour storage of, 29-30
Greasing, 122-123, 124
Grinder, Food, 54
Gravy: browning with coffee, 28; chicken, 59; correcting lumpy, 28

Ham: canned, 28-29; center cuts, 29
Hammer, as meat tenderizer, 16-17
Hamburger: and left-overs, 15; and tomato aspic, 14-15; cooking in quantity, 14; freezing of, 15; making patties, 15; pre-cooked patties, 136; stuffing peppers, 24; whipping egg white for, 15
Hydrogen Peroxide, as rust remover, 167-168

Ice Bags, *see* Plastic Bags
Ice Cream, *see* Foil

Ice Cube Trays, 50-51
Icing, Cake, 118, 120-121
Iron, *see* Cleaning, Electric Ironer
Ironing, 111-114; Ironing Men's Shirts, 114, *see also* Dampening
Ironing Board Covers, 113

Jelly Roll Tin, as drip tray, 144
Jugs, Plastic, *see* Plastic Bottles

Kerosene: removing rust with, 154; washing windows with, 141-143
Knives, sharpening of, 154

Lemon, 90-91
Lemon Juice: cleaning aluminum with, 151; cleaning copper pots with, 167; cleaning socks with, 98; in fruit pie, 127; in mashing potatoes, 71; in rice, 63; on baked potato, 73; soaking fish in, 64; tenderizing chicken with, 61; whitening breadboard with, 153
Left-Overs: freezing of, 22-23; in hamburger, 15; in meat loaf, 15; in soup, 23, *see also* Sandwich Fillings
Lettuce: coloring of, 79; drying of, 79-80; heating rolls on, 131; keeping fresh, 79; removing soup fat with, 24; separating head, 79; storing of, 80
Linoleum: as shelf lining, 6; under appliances, 146
Lint: cleaning trap, 166; making traps for, 94; removing from clothes, 166

Macaroni, 31
Magnets, for reminder notes, 157-158

177

Mayonnaise, as Jello salad topping, 22, *see also* Chicken
Meat Balls, 28
Meat Loaf: chili made from, 16; keeping from cracking, 13; with potato topping, 13; with tomato aspic, 14; with whipped egg white, 15, *see also* Left-Overs
Meringues, 129
Mop: Bleaching of, 164-165; rinsing of, 165; waxing floors with, 165, *see also* Cleaning Walls and Ceilings
Moth Flakes, 166
Muffins, 126
Mushrooms, 85

Napkin Handy Bags, 66
Newspaper Recipes, copying of, 160
Nicotine Spots, removing of, 167
Noodles: in soup, 23; with pot roast, 12
Nutcracker, 153
Nylon, *see* Washing
Nylon Net: lemon strainer, 90; potato scrubber, 145; soap bag, 145; tea bag, 155, *see also* Towels
Nylon Stocking: as lint trap, 93-94; as starch strainer, 109; to store frozen foods in, 163-164

Oleo, *see* Butter
Olives: in rice, 59; with garlic salt and oil, 24-25
Oil, Cooking: brightening kitchen shears with, 154; cleaning egg beater with, 155; removing rust with, 154
Oil, Motor: shooing flies with, 152
Onion: and cheese spread, 83; grating of, 83; in spaghetti sauce, 83; refrigerating of, 81-82

Onion Juice: making of, 83; on beef roast, 17-18
Onion Tops, as chives, 83
Orange Juice, *see* Peanut Butter
Orange Peel, as deodorizer, 47-48
Oven: cleaning of, 45-47; deodorizing of, 47-48

Pancakes, 132-134
Pans, Cooking: mixing in, 149; storing of, 6, *see also* Cleaning
Paper Plates, 159
Parsley, 84
Peanut Butter, with orange juice and vanilla, 137
Peas, Frozen: cooking of, 86; shelling of, 84
Pecans, cracking of, 137
Peppers, Stuffed, 24
Pie, 127-129
Pie Crust, 128-129
Pie Dish, as magnifying glass, 161
Pie Tin, as burner cover, 144
Pillow Slips, as chair backs, 160
Pimientos, 88
Pinch-Pleats, 100
Place Mats: covering with contact paper, 146; making from wallpaper, 68
Plastic Bags: as ice bags, 161-162; making from garment bags, 161
Plastic Bottles: keeping disinfectants in, 147; garbage catch-alls, 148; storing lettuce in 148
Plastic Containers, *see* Cleaning
Plastic Ware, *see* Cleaning
Popcorn, 27
Porcelain, *see* Cleaning
Pork, and garlic, 17-18
Pork Chops, 27
Potato: as meat loaf topping, 13; baked, 72-73; boiled-over,

75; mashed, 72; peeling of, 71, 75; refrigerating of, 76; salad, 75; sweet, 76; Three-in-One cooking of, 75
Potato Masher: as food decorator, 13; as sock washer, 99
Pudding, 121-122
Pumpkin, 76

Refrigerator: defrosting of, 48-49; deodorizing of, 52-53
Rice: burned, 63; cooking in chicken broth, 59; dry, 32; scented, 64; soufflé, 62-63; with lemon juice, 63; with olives, 59; with vinegar, 63
Roaches, 5
Rolls, 129-131
Rubber Gloves, 162

Safety Pins, in trussing turkey, 62
Saffron, 59
Salad, 39, see also Lettuce
Salad Bowl, see Cleaning
Salt, as suds reducer, 43
Sandwiches: frozen, 18, 19; wrapping lettuce and tomato, 19
Sandwich Fillings: cheese, 19; chicken, 19; egg, 19, 36; ham, 19; left-over meat, 28; meat loaf, 19
Sausage, 20, 29
Screens, see Cleaning
Shades, making of, 65
Shears, Kitchen, 154
Shellac, 158
Shelves: building of, 8-9; rearranging of kitchen, 1-9
Shishkebab Skewers, see Cleaning
Shoebag, 157
Shortening, 26, 31
Shrimp: cleaning of, 64; cooking of, 64; rice soufflé, 63

Silver, see Cleaning
Silver Polish, 158
Soap Bags, 70
Soap Film, 93, see also Electric Dishwasher
Soap Pads, 159-160
Socks, see Washing
Soup: adding spices to, 23; removing fat from, 24, see also Left-Overs
Spaghetti, 32
Spaghetti Sauce: adding onion to, 83; baking, 32; with beef, 17
Spatula, 155
Sponges, as kneeling pads, 166
Stainless Steel, see Cleaning
Starching, 107-111
Steak, see Beef
Strawberries, 89-90
Suede Brush, 156
Sugar, 134-135
Sugar, Brown, 135
Sugar, Powdered, 123
Syrup, 26

Tablecloth: drapery remnant, 67; plastic upholstery, 67; shower curtain, 67-68; terry cloth, 67
Tarnish, prevention of, 168
Tea: as beef tenderizer, 10-11; iced, 139-140; with caramel candy, 140
Terry Cloth, see Aprons, Tablecloth, Windows
Tenderizing: beef with tea, 10-11; chicken with lemon juice, 61; with hammer, 16-17
Toast, Chocolate, 25
Tomato, 85
Tomato Aspic, 14-15
Tomato Paste: in soup, 23; storing of, 85
Toothpaste, as cleaner, 169
Towels: nylon net, 69; old shirt, 69; old tablecloth, 69
Tuna Fish Soufflé, 63

Turkey: cooking of, 55-57; dressing, 57-58

Vanilla, *see* Peanut Butter
Varnish, 145
Vegetables: as snacks, 84; freshening up canned, 86-87; heating canned, 87; storing canned, 1-3
Vinegar: as laundry rinse, 93; cleaning coffee pot with, 168; cleaning chrome with, 168; cleaning oven door with, 47; in boiling potatoes, 71; in dishwasher, 41; in rice, 63

Waffle Iron, 53-54, *see also* Cleaning
Wallpaper: as place mats, 68; as shelf lining, 6, 68
Walnuts, 137
Washing: corduroy, 97; drip-dry dress, 101-103; nylon, 100; pre-rinsing, 97-98; socks, 98-100
Windows, *see* Cleaning
Waxing Floors, 165
Wax Paper: freezing hamburger in, 15; dust pan, 146; making transfers, 160-161; rolling pie crust, 128; shelf lining, 5, 9